THE GARDEN WALL

FENCES, HEDGES, AND WALLS: THEIR PLANNING AND PLANTING

Julie Harrod

Edited by Charles O. Cresson
Principal photography by Marianne Majerus
Illustrations by Rosemary Watts

THE ATLANTIC MONTHLY PRESS
NEW YORK

For Peter

Designed and produced by Johnson Editions
Ltd, 15 Grafton Square, London SW4 0DQ

Published simultaneously in Canada
Printed and bound in Hong Kong

Library of Congress Cataloging-in-
Publication Data

Harrod, Julie
    The garden wall: fences, hedges, and walls
    – their planning and planting / Julie
    Harrod
    Includes bibliographical references and
    index.
ISBN 0-87113-452-7
    1. Gardens – Design. 2. Walls.
    3. Hedges. 4. Screens (Plants)
I. Title
SB473.H38 1991 717—dc20   90-25085

American editor: Charles O. Cresson
Editor: Louisa McDonnell
Art director: Lorraine Johnson
Design: Wendy Bann
Indexer: Hilary Bird
Typesetting and artwork:
P & M Typesetting Ltd, Exeter,
Devon, England
Color separation:
Fotographics London–Hong Kong

The Atlantic Monthly Press
19 Union Square West
New York, NY 10003

First printing

· CONTENTS ·

· INTRODUCTION ·

A planting against, up, or over a wall can become a garden in itself, a rich tapestry of romantically combined shrubs, roses and vines with a long season of bloom and a surprising variety of texture and colour. And the shelter of a wall creates microclimates that can protect vulnerable plants from winter cold or excessive summer heat.

American gardeners often fail to recognize the opportunities offered by walls. In city or suburban gardens where space is at a premium, the setting for climbing and clambering plants that a wall presents is especially valuable. But for any gardener this vertical dimension provides an exciting chance to grow a range of plants unsuited to other areas of the garden.

It is no secret that *The Garden Wall* is written by an Englishwoman, Julie Harrod. She presents an extraordinary wealth of information and ideas that is equally useful to American gardeners provided it is accompanied by certain qualifications. *The Garden Wall* has therefore been extensively modified for the American edition. Even before the manuscript had been completed, I had begun to expand its scope for the North American climate, while being careful to preserve Julie Harrod's own ideas and intent. I have incorporated my own experiences across the country (and in Europe) noting regional differences as they apply to the plants being discussed. And I have tried to point out what can be grown on walls under various local conditions. The American edition includes: USDA Hardiness Zones for all plants mentioned; thoroughly edited text adapted for American gardeners; Plant Reference section revised to include varieties and cultivars for American gardeners; regional adaptability of plants.

To American gardeners *The Garden Wall* offers a wealth of ideas not only about planting but also designing and building walls, so that they complement existing buildings or garden features. There are also sections on fences and trellis, both of which provide further opportunities for growing climbing plants. Hedges too are discussed as an alternative to walls, either to enclose or divide the garden. The book is an unrivalled source of inspiration and instruction that will persuade gardeners that there is an alternative to the unimaginative bare walls or ubiquitous blankets of ivy so often encountered.

Charles O. Cresson, 'Hedgleigh Spring', Pennsylvania, 1990

· BRICK WALLS ·

English bond

Flemish bond

English garden wall

Until brick-making became a centralized industry, it was carried out on a small scale using clay from local pits. Walls constructed of such bricks have a real affinity with the underlying geology of the area and sit comfortably in the landscape. Few people nowadays can afford hand-made bricks, but modern bricks come in such a range of colours and textures that it is possible to choose a type which comes close to the brick of your region. For those who would like a wall with a more weathered appearance, the solution is to use old bricks which have been reclaimed from demolished buildings – these are often available from architectural salvage companies. Unfortunately some old bricks are softer and do not withstand frost so well as newer bricks which are fired at a higher temperature.

Most old walls were constructed from a double layer of bricks and various bonding patterns were devised to increase the strength by ensuring that vertical joints did not occur directly above one another. Medieval bricklayers, using very irregular bricks, could only use a haphazard form of bonding, but by 1500 the so-called English bond was well-established. In this pattern, a double course of stretchers (bricks lying along the length of the wall), alternates with a course of headers (bricks lying across the width of the wall).

By the seventeenth century Flemish bond, in which headers and stretchers alternate in each course, was more popular and several variations on it were also devised. Then there were English and Flemish garden wall bonds, all of which could be further decorated by the use of coloured headers produced by the action of varying temperatures and smoke on the exposed ends of bricks in wood-fired kilns.

To the modern eye, accustomed only to the monotony of stretcher-bonded cavity walls, these old patterns are rich indeed. Some people might well want to make a new wall using an old design, but it is as well to remember that the garden wall's *raison d'être* is as a support and background for plants; an intricate design may be out of place. If in doubt, choose the simplest option.

Single-thickness walls are less stable than those described above, and so must be supported by piers at regular intervals. They also afford less opportunity for decorative bricklaying unless

Stretcher bond

Flemish bond

Herringbone brickwork

Right: A new brick wall with a water feature forms a coherently integrated design. The circular frame and plain background are softened by sympathetic planting.

Centre: An unusual coping and arched recesses give a distinctive finish to a wall made with old bricks.

special half-size bricks are available. But in a small garden, such a wall is often appropriate because it is less expensive and takes up less space.

A disadvantage of new brick is that it is difficult to encourage the community of small plants that cling to the surface and root into the crevices of an old wall to such attractive effect. The spores of mosses and lichens are carried in the air and so colonization will occur eventually; but the process can be speeded up a little by coating a new wall with a thin slip of manure solution or compost water. The smell does not persist (unless you use something pungent like pig slurry), and the wall will look immediately less raw.

A double-thickness wall is not only strong, but also gives the opportunity for some decorative brickwork.

A single-thickness stretcher-bonded wall with a coping of half bricks.

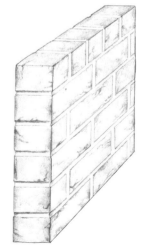

PIERS

The piers supporting a single-thickness wall (see below) make a pleasing, regular pattern that can be used to impose a degree of formality on the adjacent planting. You might plant a single shrub in each bay, or the piers could be emphasized by adding a formally-clipped evergreen in front of each one. Possible shapes include buttresses, columns or cones, depending on the plants chosen. Yew can take on almost any shape – hence its value for topiary – whereas many *Pyracanthas* would make good buttresses because of their spreading habit, while *Pittosporum*, for example, is more inclined to be conical in its natural state. Of course one can ignore the architecture of the wall entirely, but this is to waste an opportunity.

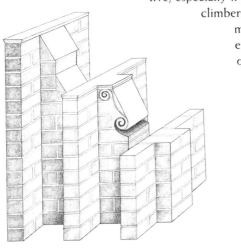

Decorative details

Most ornamentation is an intrinsic part of the wall: the pattern of the bricks, the distance between supporting piers and the choice of coping to finish the top. Some decorative features, though, such as finials and *clairvoyées*, are purely optional.

I have described bonding patterns but there are other ways of using brick to make a definite design. A honeycomb wall has a space between each brick; it is thus economical and needs fewer supporting piers than a solid, single-thickness wall of the same height because of its reduced wind resistance. A honeycomb wall is not best used as a garden boundary because of its lattice effect, but as a dividing wall within the garden honeycomb brickwork can be very attractive, especially if planted with twining climbers. These will need no more support than the existing holes and will quickly decorate both sides; the majority of the flowers, though, will inevitably appear on the sunnier side.

Herringbone brickwork can really only be used for a low wall, or a panel within a wall, but it makes an appropriate background for a small, formal planting scheme. Alternatively, its tight pattern can look most effective as a boundary to a small lawn: the zig-zag bricks contrast well with the plain sward.

There are other ways of decorating a wall beyond the more functional considerations. A hole, or *clairvoyée*, in a wall is irresistible, promising a view into some hidden landscape. If a wall is high enough to allow a hole to be placed at 1.5m (5ft) or so, no one will be able to see what lies directly beyond until they are quite close and by then the lure of the unknown will have drawn them, willy-nilly, to that part of the garden. *Clairvoyées* can be any shape – square, round, oval or even hexagonal – subject to the practicalities of building and budget. In older gardens they are often further decorated with wrought-iron work, which is especially handsome silhouetted against the sky.

A niche can provide a focal point to terminate a vista or simply a point of interest in an otherwise plain wall. It offers a chance to display a small statue or urn, but plants will not thrive unless carefully watered, because they will be sheltered from the rain. A niche is extravagant in terms of space, though, because the whole wall must

WALL ORNAMENTS
Finials and other ornaments, including urns and pineapples, can be very attractive on a large wall by a grand entrance. And on a reduced scale they can be pleasing in a smaller formal garden. But they should not be used indiscriminately, and cheap plastic-based replicas should be avoided. In most cases it is best to stick to the simplest design and repeat it only as often as is necessary for the sake of symmetry.

be set forward to accommodate it, unless the structure is particularly thick.

During the summer, properly planted and well-maintained hanging baskets are some of the brightest decorations in a garden. A house wall, especially, can easily be fitted with strong supporting brackets on which baskets can hang. There are few sights worse, though, than starved and desiccated plants in a basket, so you must be committed to daily watering and weekly feeding to keep a generous display over a long period.

Finally, a wall can support one side of a pergola. This will limit the plants one could grow actually against the wall, but in a hot climate the bowery shade offered by such a feature would be extremely welcome.

Right: A niche makes a good setting for a bust or even containers of plants. Here the architectural frame is itself loosely framed by a climbing rose.

Below: Openings in walls, whether doorways or *clairvoyées*, are always enticing, leading the visitor on to the garden or landscape beyond.

COPING

Every wall needs some sort of coping or it will look unfinished. There are many styles of coping material and if you are building from scratch it is important to investigate local variations and choose the most appealing. The simplest coping is a row of bricks set on edge; equally unostentatious are curved or bullnosed bricks specially made for the purpose, or local tiles or slates set at an angle to shed rainwater. In a more formal garden, specially made coping stones will be best. These can be obtained in various patterns – rounded, ridged or sloping – made of any number of different natural stones and stone imitations.

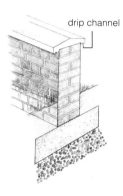

drip channel

FOUNDATIONS
A wall is only as strong as
the foundations upon
which it stands: the
concrete footings must be
at least three times the
width of the wall and in
the UK, at least 1m (3ft)
deep to extend below the
frost line (the depth to
which frost penetrates);
in colder climates the
foundations should be
deeper. Your local builder
will be able to advise what
is necessary in your
particular area.
  Care must also be taken
with the coping. It should
be a little wider than the
wall and have drip
channels, which run
beneath the coping and
carry rainwater clear of the
wall's surface.

Practical considerations
Building a new wall is an expensive
exercise and needs careful planning.
Professional advice should always be
sought, especially with regard to the
laws governing building safety and
planning permission. Be sure to consult the appropriate national or local
authority before work begins. The
house and its surroundings will suggest, if not dictate, the type of brick
and style of construction, but personal
touches can be added when choosing
the details such as coping or finials.

Bricks are manufactured in different
qualities as well as colours. They must
be reasonably weather-resistant, of
course, but if you do not want a razor-
sharp edge ten years hence then try to
choose a variety that will gradually
soften and wear. Again, the best
advice should come from your local
building store, but you should be looking for varieties of facing brick, as
opposed to engineering or common
bricks. Engineering bricks are too hard
(and too expensive); common bricks
are perfectly acceptable but are not as
finished looking as facing bricks,
whose surfaces are specially textured
to give a pleasing effect. Facing bricks
vary in strength from almost engineering quality to rather less resistant,
depending on the clay from which
they are made. Even the softer modern
bricks, though, are strong and long-
lasting; the most important point is

to find a good match for your local
brick colour.

In very straitened circumstances it
might be worth considering using concrete blocks, which are cheaper than
brick and easier to handle. The
plainest type look dull and, unless the
lumpy greyness is to be hidden
beneath rampant climbers, the wall
will have to be covered with stucco
(plaster coating). This makes a good
background for plants but it needs
maintenance and repainting which will
preclude the use of self-clinging
climbers (unless they are sacrificed
each time the wall needs attention), as
well as those shrubs which grow too
stiffly to be easily pulled away. Similar
problems occur with painted or white-
washed walls, but in a small, sunless
garden the uplifting effect of pale walls
may justify the effort of keeping them
pristine.

But there are other types of concrete block that are perfectly presentable without further treatment —
sometimes they are paler and with
attractive textured finishes. Others are
manufactured specifically to make
pierced screens that are similar to honeycomb brickwork, but much quicker
to build. Such a wall is particularly
useful in hotter climates, because it
allows cooling through-draughts. All
concrete blocks have the advantage of
relative lightness combined with
strength, and should be laid on con-

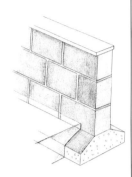

CONCRETE
A concrete block wall is
not so aesthetically
pleasing, but it is a cheaper
alternative to brick. It does
not need supporting piers
but should have strong
foundations. A simple
coping can be used —
concrete is more weather
resistant than brick.

Right: A wall of concrete blocks with a trellis extension supports climbers and shelters a plantswoman's collection of warmth-loving plants.

DAMP-PROOF COURSE

A damp-proof course above soil level will help preserve the brickwork and stop water rising by capillary action and staining the wall with salt deposits. And a wall that is as dry as possible will be much less susceptible to frost damage. Builders traditionally used three courses of engineering bricks or two layers of slate, but the modern method is simply to lay a strip of special polyethylene (or neoprene) between courses of ordinary bricks.

polyethylene (neoprene)

crete foundations as for a brick wall, but do not need supporting piers.

The height of a wall determines the amount of privacy it affords and the size of the plants that can be grown on or near it. The higher the wall, up to a limit of say 3.5m (12ft), the better and, if a choice must be made on economic grounds, opt for a short stretch of high wall rather than an insignificant wall around the whole garden. For example, it may be possible to build a high section close to the house, perhaps enclosing and sheltering a terrace area; further down the garden, where privacy is not so important, the wall could be lower.

Although there are ways of increasing the height of a low wall, for instance using trellis or pleached trees, there is nothing to beat a good high wall. The investment made will seem insignificant in the years ahead when carefully chosen and tended plants flourish in its shelter.

·STONE WALLS·

Wherever stone forms natural outcrops it is used as a building material. The traditional houses, walls and barns in such an area blend with their setting and with each other. It follows therefore that a stone wall in a clay region or a granite wall in limestone country may look incongruous.

It is easy to choose the right local material; less easy, sometimes, is to obtain sufficient quantities of stone and to find a craftsman able to use it. As old buildings and boundary walls fall into disrepair, they are sometimes demolished and the stone becomes available for re-use and may be found through architectural salvage companies; but more often today an old house will be cherished and restored. Sometimes the only option is to buy artificial stone. Types available today are hard to distinguish from the real thing and certainly easier to transport and lay.

Natural stone varies enormously, so it is not possible to make blithe general statements about a stone wall being a wonderful background for plants or being easier to colonize than brick. For instance, dark, resistant granite has a rather forbidding appearance and its hardness means that few crevices will open to allow the roots of small plants to penetrate. Choosing the right shrubs and climbers to put against granite can also be tricky: is it better to emphasize the colour by using plants with sombre leaves and dark flowers (the purist's approach but perhaps rather depressing), or to attempt to leaven the dourness with pale leaves, frothy flowers and general abandon (unfortunately rather like topping a workman's clothes with a frilly hat)?

Other dark and possibly tricky stones are flints, which are frequently used in East Anglia. Their small size, though, makes them less overpowering than granite. Slate is a dark, almost navy, blue which again is hard to plant against and red sandstone is equally difficult. Certain types of limestone are an almost aggressive orange-brown, a colour that precludes the use of anything pink in the way of flowers. White and yellow are much more harmonious.

The walls that everyone regards fondly and that are so flattering to gardens are the pale limestone walls of the English Cotswolds, for example, or, in America, of Ohio. The stone here breaks naturally into convenient, almost brick-shaped pieces and is easily

Right: An old stone and flint wall stained with lichens and supporting ivy and ivy-leaved toadflax (*Cymbalaria muralis*), is the perfect background for cottage-garden plants such as columbines (*Aquilegia*).

Below left: Elegant bearded irises looking striking against the irregular stones of a boundary wall, which has been neatly finished with a smoothly rounded coping.

Below right: Many of the rambling and climbing roses look their very best against weathered stone. Here an old wall enhances the warm colouring of the climber 'Sheldon'.

assembled in regular patterns, often without the necessity for mortar. The surfaces of these dry walls are thus ideal for small plants to colonize, while the small scale of the individual stones makes a quiet, unobtrusive background to all kinds of plants.

A limestone wall indicates an alkaline soil. The degree of alkalinity can vary from the extreme of a shallow, chalky soil to much easier loams not far from neutral, but whatever the precise conditions this is not the place to grow any of the acid-loving plants such as azaleas, rhododendrons and heathers. Choose instead from the great number of shrubs and climbers which revel in limy soil. Ericaceous plants (rhododendrons etc), come into their own in granite or slate regions.

Random stone

Flint and brick

Dry-stone
(large coping stones)

Cornish verticals

The construction of stone walls

There is little leeway in the construction of stone walls: local tradition will have devised the most efficient way of assembling the shapes of stone that occur in your region. The biggest problem, hinted at before, is finding a stonemason who can tackle the job: such craftsmen usually have more work than they can handle. Building in stone takes longer than laying bricks and there is always a certain amount of wastage, but a skilled workman will reduce this to a minimum.

Because of the expense both of the actual stone and the skilled labour necessary to use it, new stone houses are usually built with an inner skin of concrete blocks faced with stone. This idea could be copied for a garden wall, but not where an unfortunate neighbour has to look at the ugly unfinished side. It could work where the unfinished side is not overlooked directly or where it will be screened by plants.

Above ground, the construction depends entirely on the form of the stones. Reasonably flat, brick-like stones can obviously be laid in courses with little difficulty. The odd broader stone can be incorporated with some resulting irregularity in the courses, and a stable wall can be built to 1.5m (5ft) or more without using mortar. For much higher walls and in windy, exposed sites it is safer to bind the wall with cement. It might be worth considering buttresses as additional support. More rubbly stones must be laid randomly, but a course of the flattest stones can be laid every 30cm (1ft) or so to increase stability.

Flints cannot be used alone. They need the framework of quoins, usually made of brick, to support them at the corners: the bricks usually extend along the bottom and top of the wall as well.

A stone wall needs a coping as much as a brick wall, to finish it off and help protect it from the weather. Again there is a choice between the simple option of a row of stones upended or the more sophisticated effect of specially made coping stones. For a high wall, a plain coping is probably more appropriate: stones on edge can look rather busy and are better suited to lower, less impressive structures.

On the whole, stone walls pose more problems than their brick cousins: they are more difficult to build, more expensive and often more massive and therefore greedy of ground space. Before deciding to build in stone, consider the possibility of appropriate bricks. This is not such a contradiction of the vernacular as using stone where there is none, because brick has historically been used in stone areas, for precisely the reasons outlined above, and because brick is better at retaining heat than many kinds of stone, simply because it is a more porous material.

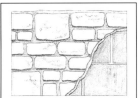

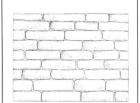

Stone-faced concrete blocks

Regular coursed stonework

Irregular courses

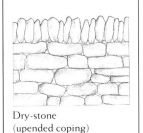

Dry-stone
(upended coping)

BUILDING A STONE WALL

A stone wall may well need stronger foundations than its brick equivalent: it is often a more massive struc-ture, usually because it has to be thicker, and because the actual stones may be denser than brick.

Completely random walls must be built with a batter (like a good hedge: wider at the bottom than the top), if they are to be safe. In any case, a random dry wall should not be built higher than 1.2m (4ft): beyond that height use mortar.

Above: The brick facing to the arches complements the superb stonework of this strongly architectural garden.

Below left: A raised terrace and a high wall of undressed stone form an impressively homogeneous unit.

Below right: This low cottage-garden wall is beautifully finished with semi-circular coping stones.

· FENCES ·

The great advantage of fences is that they are relatively cheap and quick to install; there is also a large choice of materials and styles so that it is easy to find fencing exactly suited to the site. The main problem is that the most attractive and decorative types are not completely solid; fences which do give complete privacy and seclusion are usually plain if not actually ugly. And although you can screen a fence with plants, it will have neither the strength to support the most vigorous kinds nor the sheltering warmth to allow you to grow slightly tender subjects. The need for periodic maintenance is another reason for not smothering the fence totally, even though your aesthetic instinct may suggest this.

SETTING FENCE-POSTS
Fence-posts must be firmly set. Two good methods are, to use either concrete (*left*), or special metal spikes which are inserted into a bolted metal base. Wooden posts must be treated with preservative to prevent their rotting.

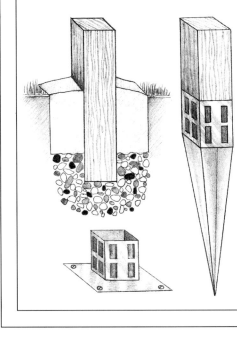

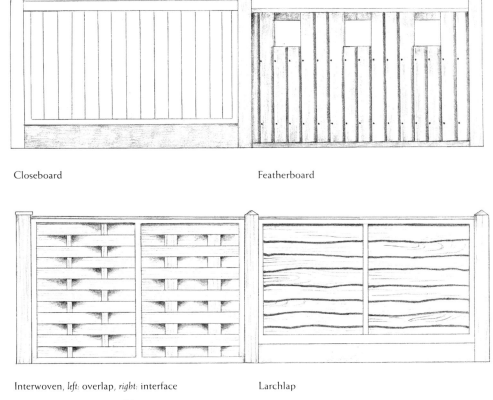

Closeboard

Featherboard

Interwoven, *left:* overlap, *right:* interface

Larchlap

Some styles of close-board fencing are more attractive than others. What is needed is a functional structure that will be strong enough to support climbers carefully chosen for their good manners and which will not blow down in the first gale. These considerations dictate that any fence be held up by strong, well-seated posts, and rule out the flimsy interwoven or lapped panels that are readily available at garden centres. Featherboard fencing is sturdier and therefore expensive, but you will find it much more satisfactory. The regular vertical lines of the pales give an uninterrupted background to planting, and the fence can be tailor-made to fit the plot. A gravel board will protect the bottom of a fence and a capping strip will save the exposed timber along the top if necessary.

For only short-term privacy, while a hedge becomes established, for instance, consider using woven hurdles made of osier or hazel, which look especially appropriate in a rural setting. They are not particularly cheap, but they are far easier on the eye than mass-produced fence panels.

There is a lot more scope when a fence is chosen for its decorative qualities rather than its contribution to privacy. These are the fences that bound front gardens and the style should ideally complement the house and garden and take into account

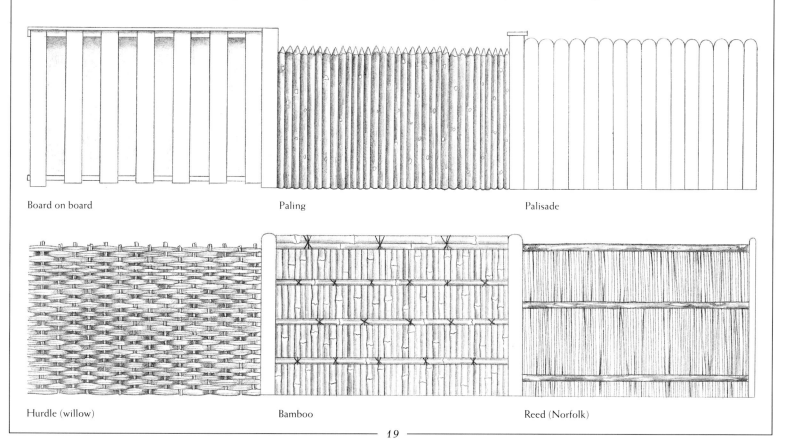

Board on board

Paling

Palisade

Hurdle (willow)

Bamboo

Reed (Norfolk)

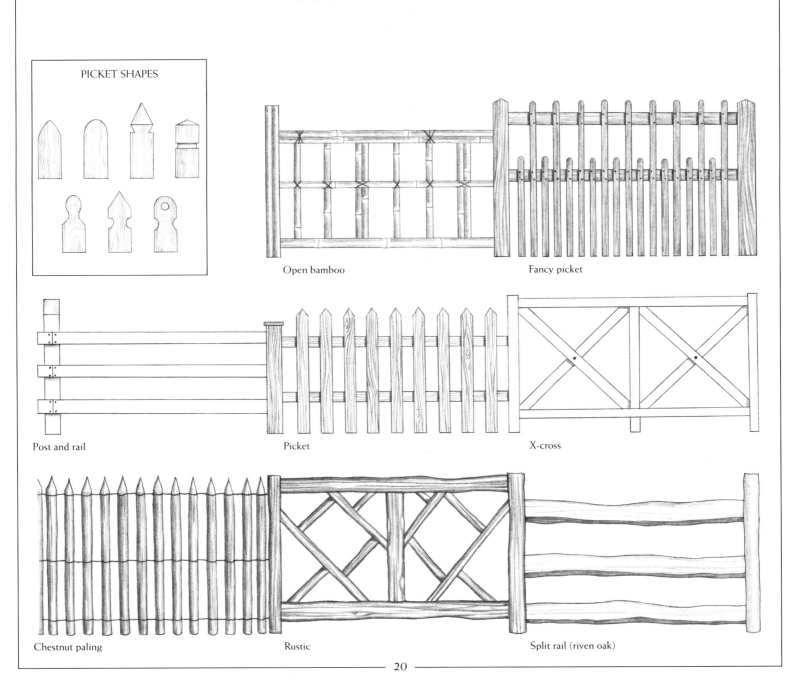

PICKET SHAPES

Open bamboo

Fancy picket

Post and rail

Picket

X-cross

Chestnut paling

Rustic

Split rail (riven oak)

the ambience of the area, but there are varieties to suit all tastes. A palisade or picket fence looks fresh, especially painted white, and it can be very formal or simply pretty, depending on the exact arrangements of the uprights and other details such as finials.

Metal fencing is also decorative and has distinct urban or rural overtones as illustrated. Think of the difference between smart spiked railings and the open style of park fencing often seen on country estates. Both types need regular painting. Chain-link fencing

is less attractive but very utilitarian, especially where a high barrier is needed. It makes frequent appearances dividing town gardens, and looks best if properly strained between firmly-set posts. Despite chain link's deceptively flimsy appearance, it makes a good support, not only for twining plants, but also for hardy shrubs which can be tied back to it, or even grown through it.

Post and rail fencing is more often seen enclosing paddocks, but where you are not concerned to keep in dogs

Below: A weathered rustic fence of posts and rails makes a discreet visual barrier in an informal garden.

Bottom: A painted picket fence of simple pattern is an ideal match for a weatherboard house

Below, right: The combination of a simple unpainted picket fence and a pergola-like construction, that supports pillar roses (short-growing climbers), draws a sharp distinction between an enclosed paved area and the large garden beyond.

or small children, it can make a sturdy, workmanlike garden boundary. Its stock-proof strength means that the rails can be easily festooned with rambling roses or other vigorous climbers that a lesser fence could not support. If the timber has been properly treated with preservative, there will be no worry about untangling everything: the fence will last for years.

Fences are less trouble to maintain than they once were, thanks to modern preservatives that protect the wood against insect and fungal attack, even below ground. The familiar smell of creosote (and all the mess that its application entailed), is now, mostly, a thing of the past. The best, and most expensive softwood timber, will have been pressure-treated with preservative chemicals, so that the wood is thoroughly protected. It is important to buy from a reputable company to make sure that this process has been adequately carried out.

The supplier will also advise on painting the timber if you do not want a natural finish. The treated wood will probably need to weather for several months before painting is possible. A painted fence will still need regular maintenance in order to keep its fresh appearance. But here too the advances in modern paints and stains mean that repainting is not nearly such a frequent chore.

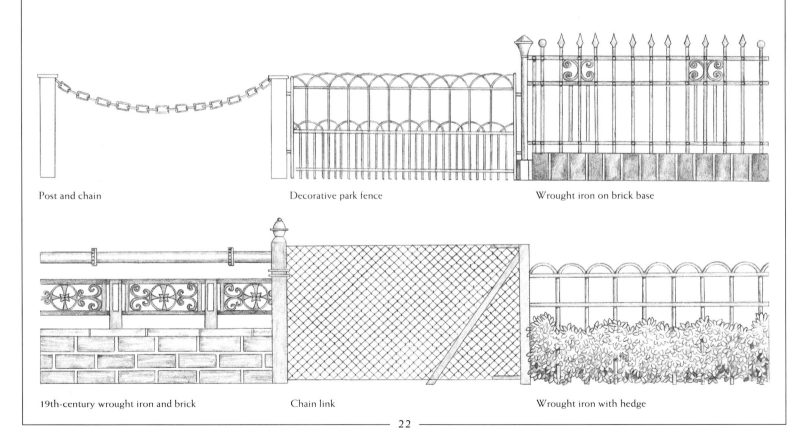

Post and chain

Decorative park fence

Wrought iron on brick base

19th-century wrought iron and brick

Chain link

Wrought iron with hedge

• TRELLIS •

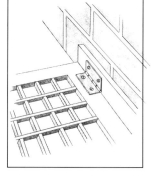

Trellis is extremely useful. Not only can it stand on its own, as a type of fence, it can also be used with existing walls and fences either as pure decoration or as a perfectly functional support for plants. Trellis is now available in a bewildering range of shapes and sizes; it has become fashionable, and the best examples are correspondingly expensive.

Do not, however, be put off considering trellis on account of expense: in some situations it is not necessary to use the costliest versions (but it is best to steer clear of the rickety expanding sort which is extremely cheap and has a very short life). To increase the height of a wall or fence all that may be needed are sturdy 60cm (2ft) panels. These prefabricated panels come in various widths and are also useful to attach to a house or garden wall as supports for climbers. They are easy to install, allow a certain amount of air circulation and certainly look better than a random arrangement of nails and wire. The natural colour of the wood fades with time and is pleasantly unobtrusive.

Specially designed trellis has a much higher profile. It comes complete with supporting posts and finials of your choice and it is strong enough to stand alone, if need be. One of the prettiest ways of using free-standing trellis is to construct a baffle, a sort of overlapping fence that makes an effective screen without the need for a gate. It should be possible to negotiate the gap easily with a wheelbarrow and the trellis can be decorated with lightweight, easily trained climbers such as clematis and honeysuckle.

When fixed to a wall, quality trellis imaginatively applied can be so decorative that you may be reluctant to hide it with plants. Special panels in teasing *trompe-l'oeil* can imitate perspective and doorways, or a trellis arch can frame an urn. These styles are for unashamedly formal gardens, but the effects are often very satisfying. If you decide to clothe the trellis (real gardeners cannot resist it), then its pleasing patterns will be revealed only in winter when they are all the more welcome.

Natural-finish trellis is available pretreated with preservative and needs little maintenance. Unfortunately, trellis designed to make a statement will need to be painted every few years – a fiddly, time-consuming task, unless

A solid architectural framework of wood has been filled in with trellis painted to match, creating a support for roses that also serves as screen and backdrop.

Top left: Despite its openness and the understated colouring of the natural wood, this fine trellis makes an impressive division, its architectural character emphasized by its height and the rounded arch.

Top right: This area for sitting out is demarcated by the decking and the pergola-like structure incorporating natural-wood trellis, which supports climbing roses more naturally than simple uprights.

Right: Trellis is a relatively cheap material from which it is simple to create a fanciful architecture, which, used with discretion, can add an intriguing dimension to a garden. The blue-green colouring of these shapes makes them distinctive but not too prominent.

A monumental gateway with broken pediment, all fashioned out of treated wood, with flanking trellis walls that are unashamedly theatrical. Hessian or netting backing to trellis is a way of creating privacy in new gardens.

you use a spray-gun, in which case it is vital to protect what lies behind from flying paint. The colour chosen will depend on the character of your garden: white is good in a shady place and always looks crisp and decisive. Green sounds like a good idea, but in fact it is hard to find a shade that neither shouts nor looks drab. The current colour in favour with designers is a greyish-blue that blends with plant tones better than might be supposed; the garden must match its formality though, or it will look merely self-conscious.

FINIALS
Finials add interest to free-standing trellis. The classic forms are spheres or obelisks, and variations thereof, but the choice of design is limitless.

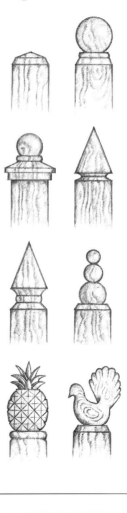

TRELLIS SHAPES
Trellis is available in varying densities. If it is necessary to hide an ugly wall or view, choose a tighter pattern than for a situation where you wish to reveal hints of what lies beyond.

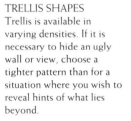

· RETAINING WALLS ·

It is difficult to garden on sloping ground, and the usual solution is to construct terraces stabilized by retaining walls. Terraces can make a plot more restful; uninterrupted slopes, although less noticeable in a large garden, are disconcerting in a smaller space.

The construction of terraces, which involves heavy earthmoving, is best done by machine, if access is possible. But the bulldozer driver must know his job or else precious top-soil will be buried leaving sour subsoil, which is not a fit medium for plants.

Retaining walls can also be used to make raised beds even in completely level gardens. Raised beds are a great help to elderly people who can no longer stoop to the ground, but plenty of youthful, able-bodied gardeners choose them because the better drainage of the elevated soil is marvellous for growing many alpines and doubtfully hardy plants. Whatever the soil of the garden, it is possible, in the limited areas of the raised beds, to add as much peat or grit or compost as is needed to make the ideal growing conditions for specially chosen plants. For example, in a cool, shady corner, a bed could be filled with an acidic peaty mixture to allow the growing of ericaceous plants; in full sun and with the addition of grit, a collection of silver-leaved plants will flourish.

The height of a raised bed should be determined by the dual considerations of utility and aesthetics. A disabled gardener may well need borders raised to half or three-quarters of a metre (20-30in) whereas 45cm (18in) will normally be sufficient from the point of view of the plants.

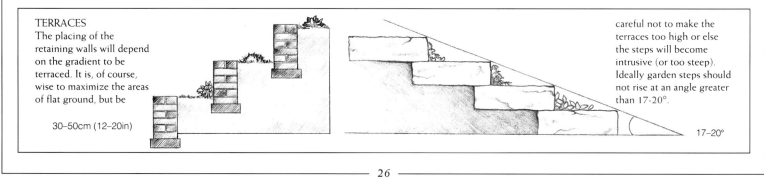

TERRACES
The placing of the retaining walls will depend on the gradient to be terraced. It is, of course, wise to maximize the areas of flat ground, but be careful not to make the terraces too high or else the steps will become intrusive (or too steep). Ideally garden steps should not rise at an angle greater than 17-20°.

30–50cm (12–20in)

17–20°

Raised beds are not simply a modern fad. For centuries gardeners have been growing plants successfully in small plots which are raised above ground level by low retaining walls. Old railway sleepers (railroad ties) make suitable walls that are easy to put in place.

THE HA-HA
The largest kind of retaining wall is the ha-ha (or sunken fence), which is only suitable for a garden with a rural outlook.

A ha-ha is a wonderful way of bounding the garden invisibly to give the effect of garden and countryside merging imperceptibly. Although it may sound rather an ambitious project, the earth can be excavated mechanically and the retaining wall, which cannot be seen from the garden, can be built cheaply and quickly using concrete blocks.

Walls that retain terraces and raised beds deserve careful thought because they certainly are visible, and may well be the dominant features of a small garden. Low raised beds may be bounded by old railway sleepers (railroad ties) whose solidity and dark colour are pleasantly unobtrusive; if it is possible to obtain them cheaply, they are ideal. In the United States landscape ties specially made for this purpose are now available.

As with boundary walls, local building materials should influence the decision as to whether stone, brick or some other material is used. There is some leeway because retaining walls are not so dominant as boundary walls and in many cases the plan is to obscure them with cascading or crevice-dwelling plants. Even so, the walls will look best if they blend with the house and surroundings: brick with brick, stone with stone.

The construction of retaining walls
Retaining walls must be strong, because the earth against which they are built is extremely heavy. Like boundary walls, they need adequate foundations, but above ground the construction techniques vary, depending on the height of the wall, whether it is made of brick or stone, and how

Low brick walls with mortared joints need trailers, such as the golden creeping Jenny (*Lysimachia nummularia* 'Aurea'), to soften the hard edges and facing.

(and if), it is to be clothed with plants.

Again brick walls are simpler to construct. If there are brick boundary walls, the retaining walls should imitate their bonding patterns. Water accumulates behind retaining walls so weep-holes (lengths of piping inserted within mortar joints) should be incorporated at regular intervals (say every 2m/6ft), about 15cm (6in) above the ground, to allow it to drain away. Because brick is a more regular and formal material than stone, attempts to grow plants in the face of the wall are apt to be unsuccessful. The best way to achieve a reasonable result is to leave spaces in the brickwork, where plants can be inserted. But it is probably better to treat the wall as a plain background; mounds of vegetation can be arranged at its foot, while trailing plants can be set at the top to cascade over the brickwork.

Stone is the better material if you intend to imitate the environment of a cliff-face with its clinging plants; dry-stone is best of all, but for a high (over 1-1.2m/3-4ft) retaining wall it is

The golden yellows of lilies and the prostrate evening primrose (*Oenothera missouriensis*), planted at the top of the this superb drystone retaining wall, are a perfect foil for the warm tones of the stonework.

BRICK RETAINING WALL

A brick retaining wall is easier to construct than a stone one, although it is less easy to grow plants in the wall face. However, trailing plants can be grown at the top and the base can be planted densely to soften the brickwork. A retaining wall should have firm foundations and should be back-filled with porous material such as pebbles or gravel to aid drainage.

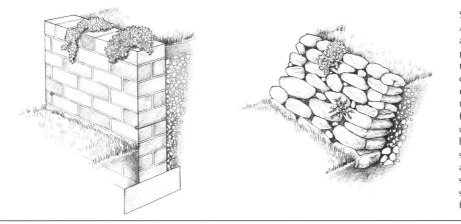

STONE RETAINING WALL

A dry-stone retaining wall is an ideal environment for plants which will thrive in the crevices; they can be chosen to complement the natural tone and texture of the stone. Large, flat foundation stones should be used to give the wall a firm base; subsequent stones should be laid at a slight angle to create a batter (a sloping face) and the wall should be back-filled very firmly.

advisable to use mortar for stability.

A fair degree of skill is required to build a dry-stone retaining wall. Each course of stones must be set a little farther from the face of the wall, giving a slight batter, and each stone should lie at an angle, the lower end being embedded in the earth. Another point to remember when building a dry-stone wall is that the earth should be rammed down absolutely firmly behind the stones. If this is not done properly, subsequent settling of the soil will weaken the wall, possibly even causing it to collapse.

Ideally, plants grown in the face of the wall should be placed as the stones are laid. In this way, the roots can be properly accommodated and the plants will make themselves at home more quickly. Trying to excavate adequate planting holes after the wall is built is very difficult and proper watering is practically impossible.

As I have already suggested, it is not easy to get plants to grow in a wall-face. A mortared stone wall will be as inhospitable as brick, but aesthetically it is much more suitable for colonization than brick, so it is reasonable to leave holes and set plants during the building. But ultimately the best way to establish plants may be to wait for them to move in themselves. Of course there must be seeds around for this to happen, so it is a good idea to set parent plants in the vicinity, perhaps in the soil above the wall, and then wait for nature's fecundity to take over. Plants that seed readily include valerian (*Centranthus ruber*), lady's mantle (*Alchemilla mollis*), *Corydalis lutea* and the small Mexican daisy (*Erigeron karvinskianus*).

Rock roses (*Helianthemum*), combined here with blue campanulas, are ideal plants to establish in sunny dry-stone walls

· GATES AND GATEWAYS ·

Unless a house stands right on the street, it is bound to have a gateway. A gate, like a front door, is in constant use and very much in the public eye, so choose it with care.

Preliminary considerations are practical: what is the largest vehicle the gateway must accommodate? A car is one thing, but what about the truck that empties the septic tank or the builder's van when you decide to extend the house? The gateway should be generous to avoid the damage that could be caused by irritated drivers trying to back through a gap which is barely wide enough. In addition to (or perhaps instead of), a large gate for vehicular access, you may want a smaller gate for pedestrians. The large and small gates should harmonize and preferably match, the smaller being a reduced version of the larger; they should also blend with the style of the house and its boundary.

There are situations in which it is not appropriate to have any gate at all; it may be better simply to frame the gap in the boundary. A gap in a wall could be defined by matching piers and finials. A hedge could be treated in a similarly formal way by allowing the end portions to grow and be clipped into simple topiary shapes.

Gates and gateways within the garden must also be practical and sited where they are needed, although they can also contribute aesthetically – for instance, to frame part of the landscape or an attractive sculpture or building. If your garden is larger than average it may have internal divisions that warrant the inclusion of extra gates (all but the smallest of gardens can appear larger by careful subdivision so that the full extent of the plot is not at first apparent). Internal gates should be as carefully considered as external ones, and the two must be related, if not identical. A garden should be a restful place, undisturbed by clashing architectural features.

Except in a very small garden an internal gateway should be wide enough to allow people to walk through two abreast; it should also be easy to negotiate with a wheelbarrow, a lawnmower and whatever other garden machinery is necessary. Any archway should be in proportion to the wall or fence, but in any case must not be less than 2m (7ft) unless it is intended to create a specially hidden place which can only be entered by stooping.

Gates can be made of metal or

PAVING A GATEWAY
A gateway should be paved: grass becomes muddy underfoot in wet weather and wears thin in summer. The paving can be done unobtrusively by setting stones or bricks flush with the lawn surface.

Above left: Paired wooden gates and trellis arches terminate each end of the short cross-axis in this garden, creating an elegant and intriguing mirror image.

Above right: This moon gate may be oriental in inspiration but the vista it frames, with trimmed box lining a gravel path that leads the eye to an impressive urn, is totally European in character.

wood. The choice of material is less important than the style of the gate: should it be formal or more rustic? In the countryside it is hard to beat the tried and tested utility of the five-bar gate. These wooden field gates can be made in different widths if necessary, and there are subtle variations in their patterns of bars and diagonals. They can be left a natural colour (properly preserved timber should need no

maintenance), or painted. For a more imposing entrance, wood can be used to make all kinds of formal patterns. Look out for local examples or find visual references in magazines or books and then find a carpenter to make up your chosen design. Where trellis has been used to create divisions it is perfectly possible to incorporate trellis gates into the design.

Some old wrought-iron gates were

Above: A solid door in a wall may be the means of creating real privacy but it can also be used as a theatrical effect to suggest a secret world on its far side.

Below: The coat of white paint saves this gate and arch from being unduly heavy but they still make an imposing entrance from the street.

extremely beautiful and ornate, but modern versions can look merely fussy, so beware. Metal might more appropriately be used to make a smarter sort of field gate with narrow rounded bars and perhaps a motif in the centre. If your garden is bounded by a hedge decide first whether to have a solid gate. A tall yew hedge gives the effect of enclosing a secret garden, and this feeling can be emphasized by using a solid door rather than a gate. Alternatively, you can offer a tempting view of the garden beyond by fitting a wrought-iron gate. A colourful flowering hedge is ornament in itself, so here it would be best to choose something unobtrusive.

Whether and what colour to paint a gate are questions that can only be answered by personal preference. Since a gate is relatively small, it is possible to use a colour that would jar if applied to an expanse of fence or trellis. A plain wooden gate could look

marvellous in bright red if it was framed by the quiet background of a yew hedge. A metal gate however, especially if it is ornate, is best painted black or very dark green. Do not forget to consider the paintwork on the house itself: if the house is visible from the gate, then the two should match or complement each other.

An opening in a high wall (or hedge or fence), can be rectangular or arched. The latter is prettier, but can only be accommodated if the wall is really high, say 3m (10ft) or more. A rectangular gateway can be made less stark by building a slight upward curve across the top, and can also be edged with a pattern of bricks or by quoins.

If a gate is fitted to the opening, remember that cold air drains downhill and if its progress is blocked by a wall or fence, then a frost pocket will result. An open-work gate will allow the air to pass through and prevent this problem.

Above: The tracery of wrought iron that fills the massive stone frame in this high brick wall makes an elegant barrier that is silhouetted against garden and sky.

Below: The tile-topped arch in this rustic rendered wall marks formally the transition from one area of the garden to the orchard beyond.

·THE WALL AS ENVIRONMENT·

The great benefits conferred by a wall are shelter and support. Although a wall may create pockets of turbulence elsewhere in the garden, the air in its lee will be relatively calm, and brittle plants or those with large or easily damaged leaves will be safe. Stone or brick reflects and absorbs heat from the sun so that a sunny wall will be warmer during the day, and through the night, as the absorbed heat is gradually dissipated.

Plants are helped in two ways by this extra warmth. The winter in the environment of the wall will be effectively less cold so it may be justifiable to risk some doubtfully hardy shrubs and climbers (see p.39). The warmer conditions also allow new shoots to ripen properly. New shoots produced in early summer are sappy and full of water; only later in the season after plenty of warmth do they harden and ripen, becoming physically strong enough to withstand the coming cold season. For plants which flower before midsummer, late summer is the time when the buds for next year's flowers (and fruit) are formed. Plants growing in a climate cooler than their native habitat will not flower generously unless there is a sheltering wall to intensify the heat of the sun.

Another, perhaps unexpected, benefit is the creation of shady areas. Plenty of shrubs and climbers are perfectly happy on the sunless side of a wall, and the ground at its foot will support a delightful community of plants, many with attractive foliage and pale, cool flowers (see p.40). The ground here can be very dry, but with suitable ground preparation and watering, it is possible to create an environment which is much more comfortable for plants than the inescapably dry, rooty shade found beneath some trees.

The support offered by a wall depends, of course, on its size. Shrubs can be trained against even a low wall, and climbers too can be accommodated, but the scope for using vigorous plants in quantity increases with the height of the wall, subject only to the gardener's ability to work from the top of a ladder or through the windows of the house.

But walls also pose problems. These are not insuperable but unless you are aware of them, the plants will not flourish as they should. The first and most important is drought. The very warmth that is so helpful to plants also increases the rate at which the soil and plants lose water by evaporation and transpiration. Furthermore, walls block out a fair amount of any rain that does fall. A high wall, obviously, is worse in this respect, and a house wall worst of all, because of its overhanging eaves. Drought problems are exacerbated by the poor, rubbly soil often found at the foot of a wall, especially around new houses. If it is hard to dig here, then plant roots will be similarly handicapped.

Frost pockets were mentioned in the section on gates (p.32), but it is worth stressing that any enclosed area will collect cold air. If the south wall is in the lowest part of the garden then tender plants may need the additional protection of sacking or bundles of straw when severe frost threatens.

The last major problem is, paradoxically, that of exposure. The walls of a house standing on a hill will have none of the cosiness of the interior of a walled garden, yet you may wish to clothe it with climbers all the same. The buffeting plants suffer will vary according to the season and the angles of the walls in relation to prevailing winds: there may be an aspect that is less difficult for plants; there will also be places where only the hardiest plants, strongly attached to the wall, will make any progress.

Overcoming drought
Drought poses the biggest threat to

Opposite: Many plants that would not flourish in the open garden will do well and flower freely if grown against a warm wall. In cool temperate climates the magnificent but tender *Fremontodendron californicum* needs such a position.

Below: Even on the shady side of a wall there are plants that will grow happily. Foxgloves (*Digitalis purpurea*) and *Corydalis lutea* self-seed freely.

plant growth against a wall, and this is true of any aspect.

As with most matters pertaining to gardening, the key to success lies in the soil. It is crucial to water newly-set plants until they are established, but the aim also must be to make the soil so rich and water-retentive that more than average irrigation is unnecessary thereafter. Water is held in the soil by organic matter, so as much of it as possible should be incorporated.

Organic matter comes in many

forms. Most people think first of peat, which is weed-free, easy to handle and readily available, but it is by no means the perfect soil conditioner. It is expensive and, to plants, nutritionally worthless so that some kind of fertilizer must also be incorporated. It is also, despite its great water-holding capacity, very difficult to thoroughly dampen once it has dried out. A lot of water must be stirred in and then left to be absorbed before the peat is fit to use: dry peat dug into a dry border will do no good at all unless some heavy and prolonged rain conveniently falls soon afterwards. For environmental reasons too, gardeners should look elsewhere for their organic matter, because peat is being used at such a rate by the horticultural trade that reserves are being severely depleted (peat forms extremely slowly). Try, therefore, one of the alternatives listed below.

A 'crinkle-crankle' wall is unfortunately particularly expensive to build and is space consuming, but the recessed sections on the sunny side provide very sheltered and warm conditions for choice and tender plants.

Gardeners in stock-producing rural areas should have little difficulty in obtaining farmyard manure. This varies in its nutritional content and can be difficult (not to say smelly) to handle, but it is cheap and plentiful. It will probably contain weed seeds but these are easily killed by a contact or pre-emergence herbicide which acts when the seeds germinate. After using a herbicide it may be necessary to wait a while before planting: refer to the manufacturers' instructions. Spent mushroom compost is also available in some areas and is excellent for improving the soil.

Even in towns gardeners can manage without peat, because there are various brands of commercially prepared and specially concentrated forms of organic matter that are preferable. They are cleanly packed in bags, are free of weeds and have the advantage of containing plant nutrients, although the amounts of these may vary widely.

Do not forget ordinary garden compost. A compost heap or bin can be fitted into all but the tiniest garden; compost can even be made in black dustbin liners (plastic garbage bags). Unless it is very carefully made, it will contain weed seeds and fragments of weed roots, but the roots can be removed by riddling and the germinating seedlings can be killed by an appropriate herbicide or by the simple expedient of several cultivations over the growing season.

Having dug out obstructing stones, rocks and lumps of mortar, and conditioned the soil with masses of organic matter, one can think about setting the plants. Even after adding organic matter to the whole border, I still like to use some in the individual planting holes. Many plants today are sold in containers so their roots suffer little disturbance at planting, but if (as is usual), they have been grown in soil-less compost then the shock of encountering real soil can be severe. Soften the blow by digging a hole larger than the container and mixing garden compost (or whatever you are using), with the soil at the bottom of the hole.

Any plant which has been too long in its pot should have its coiled roots gently teased out before it is set, and if the compost seems at all dry dunk the pot in a bucket of water and leave it until air bubbles have stopped escaping. Unless the soil is very wet, water generously; if the soil is dry, water it thoroughly the previous day and put plenty of water in the planting hole and over the firmed earth to get rid of air pockets around the roots. After planting, the best way to reduce water loss is to apply a mulch – a 5cm (2in) layer of, say, chipped bark or rotted lawn clippings – around the plant. An obvious point, but one that is often forgotten, is that the plants should be positioned at least 30cm (1ft) (and preferably a little farther), out from the base of the wall. As they grow, they can easily be trained in the right direction using sticks and string.

Some houses are surrounded by paving, in which case the only way to use the walls to support plants is to grow them in containers. These must be as large as can be afforded or there is space for, and must be filled with good quality compost with a high organic content. Even so, watering will be a constant chore during the warmer months, but the range of plants which can be successfully grown in containers is large and varied: all the effort will be amply rewarded.

Winter poses a different problem, because the soil in containers will freeze easily and only the hardiest of plants can be expected to survive. In cold climates, containers must be moved into a frost-free building for the winter; in areas where the weather is less extreme, plants can be protected during a cold snap by wrapping the container with insulating material or sinking them into mulch. It may be helpful to think of the root systems of plants as being a zone or two less hardy than the aerial parts.

House, garden and retaining walls compared

For several reasons house walls present the greatest challenge to the gardener.

Even when a house has the benefit of generous borders all around it, there will be few stretches of wall that are not punctuated by a door or window. Other interruptions may include drainpipes and central heating flues. The actual wall area available for planting is restricted to the spaces in between, which tend to be tall and narrow however large the house may be. Such spaces are far from ideal for plants such as roses which flower more freely when their shoots are trained horizontally. So to clothe a house wall effectively it will be necessary to use several types of plant: low shrubs beneath the windows, larger shrubs or well-mannered climbers between windows and doors, together with more vigorous (but carefully trained), climbers reaching towards the roof.

A house that is stuccoed or painted must be treated differently because of the need for periodic maintenance, when all the plants must be removed. Self-clinging climbers or anything too aggressively prickly are not, therefore, desirable. And of course a house of great architectural merit should not be hidden by unrestrained greenery.

Garden walls are much less restrictive because they offer an unbroken planting space. Some people may even be lucky enough to have an adjoining barn (or similar out-building), in which case there will be a wall about the same height as the house but with-

A rough stone retaining wall is planted with easy hardy plants, such as the white form of valerian (*Centranthus ruber*), aubrietas and pinks (*Dianthus*) as well as more tender plants such as *Convolvulus cneorum*.

out all the interruptions. Even low garden walls offer some support and shelter, although the scale is smaller.

Since retaining walls are lesser features, they naturally support correspondingly smaller plants, but their construction offers special advantages. The earth at the top of the wall is well drained (because it is raised), and provides an ideal situation for plants that cannot stand being waterlogged. Plants growing in the face of the wall will have even drier surface conditions. They are forced to grow at an angle, thus throwing off any rainwater, and there is no cold wet soil around their necks in the winter; in summer their roots are kept cool behind the stones.

Not all retaining walls are suitable for alpine treasures, though, because aspect, rainfall and the prevailing wind are important too. A shady, damp wall face will be a much better home for ferns and mosses, so accept this and make a collection of cool greenery. At the other extreme, a garden may be in an arid area where only succulents have a chance to survive, especially in the even drier conditions of a wall.

The type of stone and overlying soil of an area may be acid, alkaline or roughly neutral, and this affects the choice of plants: pinks and gypsophila, for instance, like lime, whereas most of the precious blue gentians need acid conditions. Again, it is foolish and ultimately unsuccessful to fight nature.

· THE IMPORTANCE OF ASPECT ·

The direction in which a wall faces is one of its most important characteristics and it should be planted accordingly. In cool areas, a south or south-west facing wall is always to be coveted because of the shelter it affords to marginally winter-hardy plants. It is worth noting, though, that the plants that most need the extra warmth tend to be shrubs rather than climbers. As is explained later in the book, there are many worthy shrubs that should not be risked except in the shelter of a south wall, whereas climbers are for the most part equally happy facing west.

In cool regions shoots ripen more easily near the warmth of a wall and will bear more flowers and fruit, so space on a south wall is in demand not only for ornamental plants, but also for fruit trees, especially the more tender varieties like peaches, nectarines, apricots and figs. A south wall may have the drawback of encouraging plants into growth early, leaving new shoots and blossom susceptible to late frosts, so in an unpredictable climate, a gardener must be ready to protect vulnerable blossom if frost threatens. A different problem arises in warmer areas, where a south wall may reflect too much heat for heat-sensitive plants; here, a partly shaded wall is preferable for many plants.

At the foot of a south wall, the soil will be hot and dry in summer: ideal conditions for several kinds of bulb that originate in warmer climates. The Algerian _Iris unguicularis_, can be shy to flower in the open, but if it has a summer baking it is likely to produce a long succession of pale purple flowers in early spring. The lovely Guernsey lilies (_Nerine_ spp.), are welcome in October and unexpectedly exotic looking as winter approaches: they too will thrive below a south wall.

The base of a south-facing wall is an especially valuable warm position for planting. The spires of _Acanthus latifolius_ mingle with those of hollyhocks (_Althaea rosea_).

A north wall is often feared by gardeners new to the game. But there are plenty of perfectly hardy shrubs and climbers from which to choose, and some of the most effective garden compositions can be made here. Some climbers – honeysuckles, for instance – positively prefer shade, being in nature inhabitants of woodland, and are ideal. There are many shrubs, hydrangeas among them, that grow best out of the direct heat of the sun, and also plenty of shade-loving herbaceous plants, including the aristocratic hellebores and hostas. Bulbs suitable .for a north wall include snowdrops (*Galanthus* spp.), *Anemone nemorosa*, crocuses and bluebells (wood hyacinths). A north wall deserves to be coveted too. Do remember that this aspect can be dry also, so soil improvement and initial watering are vital to the success of the plants.

A wall facing west will, in the British Isles, receive the full benefit of the prevailing wind and the rain it carries so plants growing here will be able to establish more quickly because of the damper soil. A west wall also enjoys the warm rays of the afternoon sun and thus comes close to a south wall in providing shelter for slightly tender plants, especially since the late afternoon heat is held by the wall and re-radiated through the night.

An east wall has one particular danger in winter and spring: morning sun will shine directly on cold leaves, stems and flowers, warming them too rapidly and causing unnecessary damage. Evergreen foliage burns badly in cold climates under these circumstances; flowers of early blooming shrubs are easily withered by such rapid temperature changes after a frosty night. Camellias or wintersweet (*Chimonanthus praecox*) cannot be risked, even though they may be perfectly hardy plants, because it would be heartbreaking to see them with tattered browned flowers. A wind from the east is usually cold, so plants for this aspect must be hardy.

Having read this, you may discover that your wall is not aligned with any cardinal compass point but instead faces roughly north-east or approximately west south-west. Another possible complication might be the presence of overhanging trees (outside the garden and hence your control), which cast shade. A shaded south wall will be less useful as shelter for tender plants because it is the sunlight itself, concentrated by the wall, that is important, but it will still be warmer than a north wall. In the last analysis, only you can assess the characteristics of your particular wall and make educated guesses as to what might grow well against it. And, of course, experimentation will provide the ultimate answers.

Above and right: In this Australian garden the walls flanking a pathway provide a cool environment where temperate-climate plants such as wisteria and roses thrive.

with good foliage to grow at the foot of the wall and, where appropriate, in the wall face.

The remarks about east and west aspects apply equally to retaining walls, with commonsense provisos: since alpines dislike being water-logged, it is foolhardy to risk them on a drenched windy wall in the west of Ireland, for instance. And the danger of combined sun and frost damage is reduced on small walls, simply because most of the plants that may be used come into flower after the severest frosts have passed.

Aspect also affects the character of retaining walls. Many alpine plants need maximum light and in cool moist climates will not thrive except on a south wall. They do not so much need the summer heat as dry, bright conditions in winter to prevent them rotting; hence the need for the sunny aspect. A retaining wall that does not get the sun can be a problem if the aim is to clothe its face with trailing plants set at the top, because most plants simply will not trail into the shade. Instead, they strain toward the sun and any growth that does fall down the wall carries flowers only sparsely. A shady retaining wall will therefore probably be most successful if plants that actively enjoy being cool are used. Forget about trying to mask the top and concentrate instead on plants

·PLANTS FOR WALLS AND FENCES·

Climbers

Plants cannot live without light. In their quest to trap the sun's energy different sorts of plants have developed various strategies: trees and shrubs make woody tissue to support their aerial growth, while annual weeds simply produce phenomenal quantities of seed so that any open patch of ground can quickly be colonized. Climbing plants rely on trees and shrubs for their support and, being freed from the necessity to make strong stems, they are often able to spread rampantly.

Climbers do their climbing by various means and it may be useful to consider them as separate groups. This classification is artificial and some of the boundaries (such as between the twiners and the scramblers), are blurred, but in general the distinctions are helpful, because they enable you to choose the best way to attach them to your wall or fence.

Climbers with tendrils

Plants with tendrils are easy to recognize. They include well-known climbers such as the grape-vines, the pea family and the passion-flowers. Tendrils are modified leaves that remain straight until their questing tips

The tendrils of passion-flowers cling firmly to a wire support.

'feel' the presence of a possible support. The tendril then curls quickly around the support and takes a firm hold. Tendrils give these climbers a certain delicacy of appearance coupled with firmness once they are established. It is difficult to unwind a tendril without destroying it.

The grape-vines (*Vitis* spp.), are particularly ornamental, many varieties having the dual attractions of distinctive leaves (often with good autumn colour), and attractive (and usually edible), fruit. On a warm wall, it is worth trying *Vitis* 'Brant', whose tiny, very sweet black grapes are almost scented, and so delicious that very few will get as far as the table. Brant's foliage turns bright red in autumn. *V. vinifera* varieties grow best on the Pacific coast of the United States; in the east the native foxgrape, *V. labrusca* varieties are better. 'Concord' is traditionally the most popular, but many white, red and purple varieties, some seedless, are available.

A more vigorous vine, and one that is grown purely for decoration, is *Vitis coignetiae*, whose distinction lies in its huge leaves. These are jaggedly heart-shaped and they turn warm orange and red in autumn. Because of its large

Opposite: Clematis, which are deservedly among the most popular flowering climbers, use twining leaf stalks to hoist themselves up. In addition to the many large-flowered hybrids there are several species and near species that are good garden plants. *Clematis alpina,* for example, is one of the best of the shorter-growing species and suitable for a small garden. Most forms have violet or purple flowers; in this respect 'White Moth' is untypical.

Below: The vigorous vine *Vitis coignetiae* is a spectacular climber. Here its large leaves frame a terracotta urn surrounded by bergenias.

Top left: The brilliant autumn colouring of _Vitis coignetiae_ seems luminous beside the sombre purple tones of _V. vinifera_ 'Purpurea'.

Top right: An easy and vigorous species, _Clematis montana_ has several forms with a colour range from white to purplish red.

Below: On the wall rose, clematis and vine (_Vitis coignetiae_) interlace, as climbers often do, to form a harmonious combination of foliage and flower.

scale, this is a plant to grow on a high wall where it can spread freely; it can be grown in a more restricted space but will need repeated cutting back and, unless this is done skilfully, the result will be an ugly mess.

There are several kinds of passion-flower, of varying degrees of hardiness. On a warm wall (zones 7-8), it should be possible to grow _Passiflora caerulea_, probably the best-known variety, with its distinctive blue fringe to the complicated flowers. 'Constance Elliott' is an ivory white, with yellow anthers. The dark green, lobed leaves are pleasant enough, but passion-flowers are often shy to bloom, even in a very sheltered place. Generosity of flower production is in part genetically determined and since many passion-flower plants are raised from seed they show a wide variation in their ability

to flower freely. Named varieties should be vegetatively propagated and thus more reliable in this respect. The Maypop (_P. incarnata_), native of the south-eastern United States, is the hardiest species. Its flowers are somewhat smaller but still quite showy. It is a herbaceous perennial that dies to the ground in winter but rapidly grows to 6m (20ft) by late summer; the spreading rhizomatous roots are easily controlled in northern areas.

Eccremocarpus scaber is a smaller climber which also likes a warm situation. Its leaves are small and ferny and the tubular orange flowers appear in late summer. It can be grown from seed (started with some heat in spring), to clamber over other wall shrubs or climbers, or to cover trellis: it is particularly pretty on trellis because of its delicate appearance and

ease of training. It is also an ideal plant to use as a space-filler, perhaps where another climber has died, or in a new garden where all the recently-set plants are still too small to be significant. Unfortunately, this is a climber that resents hot summers and does not do well in hotter regions in the eastern United States.

Clematis
The clematis family is large and varied (they are mainly climbers, but there are some herbaceous types as well), with at least a score of species and over 50 large-flowered varieties; there is obviously not space here to include them all, but to ignore them altogether would mean passing over some of the showiest and most beautiful climbers. These use their leaf stalks (petioles) rather like tendrils. The petioles wrap around the support and, like tendrils, are not easily unwound. As clematis grow rapidly, they should be regularly trained to prevent dense tangles from forming.

As a rule, clematis prefer alkaline conditions but as long as they have a deep, moist root run they will grow in any good garden soil. They are essentially woodland plants, equipped to scramble up into trees, and in such conditions the soil is hardly ever in direct sunlight. A far cry, in fact, from the average garden where the foot of a wall or fence can be very hot indeed,

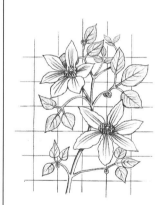
Clematis climb by means of twining petioles (leaf stalks).

so it is especially important to shade the roots with stones or a good thick mulch. It is also important to plant clematis deeply, with a few centimetres of stem below soil level. This is a precaution against clematis wilt, a disease whose cause is still unknown, which attacks the stems at the soil surface and can collapse the entire plant in a matter of days. If part of the stem is buried, new roots will form here and the plant will be able to send up shoots from underground buds and make a fresh start.

With some exceptions, clematis are not actually good plants for growing directly onto a wall because their growth is too insubstantial and they tend to be leggy at the bottom and to produce most of their flowers in a bunch at the top. This tendency can be useful in some situations, though; you can have flowers decorating a sunny top of a wall by setting a clematis on the shady side and allowing it to grow up and over into the light. Those that make a better job of covering are the several varieties of *Clematis montana*, which can reach 6 or 9m (20 or 30ft) with the help of supporting wires. They grow quickly, need no pruning and in May and June are literally covered with flowers. I particularly like the plain white 'Grandiflora'; the slightly later variety, *wilsonii*, has similar flowers but these have the added attraction of scent. Other varieties

'Duchess of Albany' is a hybrid clematis with *C. texensis* in its parentage. It dies down almost completely in winter but grows annually to a height of about 3m (10ft).

have flowers ranging from pale to deep pink, and 'Tetrarose' has bronzy foliage to set off its lilac-pink blooms.

Earlier in spring, *Clematis macropetala* is a lovely thing with its ferny, divided foliage and drooping, double flowers. This is a much less vigorous species than *C. montana* and can safely be used in a smaller space: it looks particularly pretty grown through trellis. I remember once seeing it scrambling up beside an arched gateway beyond which (some distance away), there stood a big copper beech. Just as the beech leaves were unfolding, during the precious week when the foliage was still a wonderful translucent red, the slaty blue clematis flowers were perfectly emphasized. 'Markham's Pink' is another variety of *macropetala* and 'White Moth' is a very similar plant, actually a variety of *C. alpina*; you can create a more unusual picture by growing the different colours together. No pruning is necessary.

You will find some of the later species clematis described in the section on Plant Combinations (see p.83). Others worthy of mention include the semi-herbaceous variety *Clematis × jouiniana* 'Praecox'. This will not climb on its own but the plentiful stems are easily tied to a support and its small, purple-edged white flowers are produced in great profusion from late summer. It looks particularly effective with other silver and purple plants,

such as *Buddleia* 'Lochinch' which has felty grey leaves and long, elegant violet-blue inflorescences. It can be used as a free-standing shrub but a wall will give it extra warmth and shelter and

Left: Although semi-herbaceous, *Clematis × jouiniana* 'Praecox' can be trained against a wall where it will benefit from the extra warmth and shelter.

Below: The large-flowered clematis, 'Henryi', does well on any aspect; here it makes a cool picture teamed with the rose 'Iceberg'.

you should get flowers slightly earlier in the season.

The large-flowered clematis are numerous and diverse. Colours range from white through pink and red to deep purple, and the flowers may be single or double. The best way to choose is to visit a good nursery to observe the habit of the individual plants (see p.155 for some suggestions) as well as discover their true colours: even good printing cannot reproduce these accurately, especially the slight differences which distinguish the varieties in the 'blue' part of the colour range. The intricacies of pruning are explained later in the book (see p.146).

Self-clingers

Plants in this category are often slow to begin climbing: their roots seem to need time to become established before the aerial parts move at all, but once they do settle down to grow they become large and immovable, so they are obviously unsuitable for a fence. Although they do indeed fasten themselves to a surface, they will probably need initial support to encourage them to grow in the right direction and to keep the shoots still enough to make firm attachments to the wall. They may also need some tying in as they grow and mature. Even with these, the most self-sufficient of climbers, it is necessary to make some effort to help

Ivy is a self-clinger which attaches itself to walls by means of aerial roots

them grow in the desired fashion.

The ivies (*Hedera* spp.), in all their wonderful variety of leaf, offer a huge range of possibilities. Some kinds are small-leaved and diminutive, others vigorous with large, flamboyant leaves to match; some are extremely hardy, even in the north (zone 5) and not at all fussy about soil. Perhaps because of their very ease of cultivation some people regard them with scorn, but this is to do these versatile plants an injustice. A visit to a specialist nursery is the best way to choose exactly the right plant; failing that, an illustrated catalogue from such a supplier should be convincing proof that ivy does have a place in the garden.

Above and below: The many cultivars of the common ivy (*Hedera helix*) vary greatly in leaf shape, size and colour. The golden and variegated forms are especially good on dark walls.

The parthenocissus family is another group of plants which has suffered the epithet 'common' or, equally damning, 'suburban', but these climbers too deserve consideration before moving on to more esoteric (and tricky), plants. In England, the common name Virginia creeper seems to be used for both *Parthenocissus quinquefolia* and *P. tricuspidata*, although the latter should be known as Boston ivy; its palmate leaves are roughly similar to those of ivy, whereas the creeper's leaves are five-lobed and hence more delicate in appearance. Both plants have had the misfortune to be used indiscriminately on red brick walls, where they look perfectly fresh and green throughout the summer but where their autumn colours of riotous crimson and scarlet are totally wasted in a vain battle with their unsympathetic background. A third member of the family is less often seen, although it has more distinction: *P. henryana* has three- or five-lobed leaves which are decorated with silver and pink veins. It also colours well in autumn.

On the whole I rate these plants less highly than the ivies although they are equally tolerant of shade and poorish soil; this judgement is based solely on the grounds that they are deciduous. A parthenocissus grows to fill a large expanse of wall and this is then completely denuded throughout the winter. In a small garden the luxury of such a

waste of space cannot be afforded.

If you have a sheltered, sunny position, and are keen to try something out of the ordinary, *Trachelospermum jasminoides* is an evergreen whose leaves are dark and glossy, in attractive contrast to its creamy flowers. As the name suggests, these look like jasmine – and have an equally sweet scent. There is a related species, *T. asiaticum*, which is very similar and somewhat hardier, but its flowers are smaller. Both could be lost in a bad winter, but this is true of many tender plants and should not deter you from trying one or the other.

Twiners

Some plants twine more recognizably than others. This group inevitably

The twining stems of the star jasmine (*Trachelospermum jasminoides*) have been trained here as an arch over a doorway so that the delicious scent of the small white flowers can charm one into the garden.

Honeysuckles are twiners that will climb easily up a trellis.

slides into the last category, the scramblers and thorn-bearers, but there are enough out and out twiners for the distinction to be valid: they include the well-known honeysuckle, jasmine and wisteria.

Wisteria is an aristocrat amongst climbers, but it is a plant which needs space to look its best. A well-trained specimen in full flower against pale stone is indeed a thing of beauty, but do not be bewitched into trying to grow it in too small a garden. For one thing, it may take several years to begin to flower and in the meantime it will send its pliant green stems in all directions if it is not pruned and trained carefully. And in the southern United States it can be especially rampant. Select one or two shoots and tie them horizontally, and then cut back the rest to 2cm (³/4in) or so, in summer. This will check the plant's vigorous growth and encourage it to form flower buds. It is worth pointing out that a newly planted wisteria may be reluctant to come into leaf in its first spring if it becomes at all dry, so pay special attention to watering.

The two main species come from Japan and China: the forms of the Japanese *Wisteria floribunda* tend to have much longer flower trusses than those of *W. sinensis*. These can look extravagantly beautiful or merely overblown, depending on the scale of the background, so do not be seduced by cata-

logue pictures or descriptions into planting *W. floribunda* 'Macrobotrys' (whose flowers grow in huge racemes up to 90cm/3ft long), unless you really can accommodate it.

The honeysuckles will be described later (see pp.54–5), because they come into the category of 'good rent-payers' as an elderly gardening friend once described those useful plants which are almost indispensable, especially in a small garden.

The large impressive leaves of *Aristolochia*

The Japanese wisteria (*W. floribunda*) is less vigorous than the Chinese species (*W. sinensis*) but can still reach a height of 9m (30ft). 'Rosea', shown here, is one of several cultivars.

Here the yellowish leaves of the golden hop (*Humulus lupulus aureus*) provide a lovely background for bearded irises and foxgloves.

Jasmine (*Jasminum officinale*), one of the most sweetly scented of summer flowers, blooms freely when grown against a sunny wall.

macrophylla, syn. *A. durior* (commonly known as Dutchman's Pipe), make an excellent cover for a wall. The flowers are tubular and yellow-green and they appear in early summer, but it is the somewhat rough, heart-shaped leaves which are the main attraction. Too coarse, probably, for a small garden, but nevertheless worth considering for an otherwise featureless expanse of wall.

In contrast, the foliage of *Akebia quinata* is most delicate, each compound leaf composed of five leaflets. Again, this is the plant's best feature although there are fragrant purple flowers in late spring and purple sausage-shaped fruit in autumn, but the fruit is only produced if the spring and summer have been hot and sunny. The related *A.trifoliata* has only three leaflets per leaf but it too makes a pleasant mass of delicate green. Both are semi-evergreen, keeping their leaves in a mild winter.

The hop (*Humulus lupulus*), is actually a herbaceous plant, dying to the ground in winter and making its prodigious growth – up to 4m (14ft) or more – during the summer. The ordinary green form is attractive enough with its jagged three-lobed leaves and pale green papery hops (on female plants) in late summer, but it is the golden-leaved variety which is most eye-catching. The yellow colour develops best in a sunny position.

The scent of jasmine is sweet, the very breath of summer, likeable too for its neat, dark green, pinnate leaves which are so prettily pointed. It needs a warm wall to flower freely and it can grow to 3m (10ft) and more, but its green stems are easy to cut back and the plant can be kept within the bounds of a small garden. There is a selected form, *Jasminum officinale affine*, which.has larger flowers with a pink tinge on the outside.

Scramblers and thorn-bearers

These are all plants which need firm tying in to their support. This is not to say that the climbers mentioned before need less maintenance, simply that the scramblers have less inclination to climb and many of them would happily make huge mounds upon the ground or heave themselves over other plants rather than reach for the sky.

The potato family includes several climbers whose flowers are pleasantly familiar from the vegetable garden. *Solanum crispum* 'Glasnevin' needs a sheltered, sunny wall where it will grow quickly and produce masses of purple, yellow-centred flowers in loose inflorescences over a long period from summer into the autumn. It is semi-evergreen, but is not particularly attractive during the winter. A similar species, *S. jasminoides*, has a white-flowered form which is I think prettier. This will actually climb by twining, but it too needs a warm wall.

Celastrus orbiculatus both twines and bears small thorns. It is a thug, only suitable for a big space or to cover an ugly building, but it does give a marvellous display of colour in the autumn. Good nurseries sell hermaphrodite plants that are self-fertile (otherwise you will need both male and female plants, and few gardens can accommodate more than one *Celastrus*), and these produce generous quantities of fruit. The seed capsules are brown-yellow splitting open to reveal bright red seeds similar to the fruit of the spindle tree (*Euonymus europaeus*), which belongs to the same family. Set in a background of yellowing leaves, these points of colour make a memorable picture. Since the plant is so vigorous, you will be able to cut armfuls of the stuff to decorate the house without spoiling what is left.

Annuals

Most climbers are large, fast-growing plants, but many take at least one season (and sometimes more), to become settled and established before making substantial upward progress. If you plan to live in your house only for a year or two and you want to enjoy well-clothed boundaries then you should choose some of the precocious annual climbers as well as plants for more permanent interest.

Annual nasturtiums are usually allowed to trail along the ground but they can just as easily be encouraged to climb and are very useful to fill a gap for a season after the loss of a plant, or in a new garden. Simply push the fat seeds into the ground where you want them to grow and then thin and train as necessary. The plants will seed themselves, so in subsequent years you need only move or discard the offspring if they appear in the wrong place. Nasturtiums are attractive fodder for certain kinds of caterpillar. One

'Glasnevin' is the most commonly grown cultivar of *Solanum crispum*. Although an ungainly plant, it flowers prolifically.

The white-flowered form of the potato vine (*Solanum jasminoides* 'Album') is a lovely airy plant that performs well in late summer.

year my plants were so disfigured that I had to pull all of them out. I threw them on the compost heap, where they promptly began to make new roots along the stems, demonstrating how tough and easy to grow they are.

The morning glories (*Ipomoea* spp.), are beguiling relatives of that appalling strangler, bindweed, and the open flowers, especially of the cultivar 'Heavenly Blue' are extremely beautiful. The seeds are easy to germinate on the kitchen window-sill but much more difficult to grow on, because the seedlings will be set back by any suggestion of cold or overwatering. They may survive, but flowering will be delayed. The flowers, when they do appear, are indeed lovely, but each one lasts barely six hours and in the afternoon and evening there is nothing glorious about the plants at all. So plant morning glory if you are a lark as opposed to an owl by nature, and if you have the sheltered position it needs to look its best. Trellis provides good support for the twining stems: a wall is too solid a background for so insubstantial a plant.

Much more dramatic and altogether a better choice is *Cobaea scandens* (hardy perennial in zone 9). The seed germinates better if each one is sown on its side, which is hardly a difficult procedure but worth the small extra effort. It needs strings or wire to scramble up with its adhesive tendrils, or you can

Pink and mauve morning glories (*Ipomoea*) are in their element scrambling among the dark red flowers of *Bougainvillea* in a Spanish garden.

Sweet peas (*Lathyrus odoratus*) give a wonderful return of pastel-coloured fragrant flowers if they are grown in a rich soil and well watered.

let it grow over and down a retaining wall; in this way the profusion of intricate bell-shaped flowers – purple with hints of green and cream – can be seen at close quarters. As with all plants that make a lot of growth quickly, it needs good soil and plenty of water.

For a smaller space in regions with cool summers, say against a raw new fence, it is hard to beat the ordinary sweet pea, grown through unobtrusive strings or wide-meshed netlon. The seed can be sown in autumn in pots for an early summer display, but spring-sown plants grow quickly in any case. Sweet peas like moisture and plenty of compost or well-rotted manure at their roots, so a trench should be excavated along the line of the fence and as much as possible of this material added, well before planting time. I did this in a tiny town garden and was thrilled with the result. There was space in the narrow border to set other

plants to clothe the bottom portion of the peas, and above this, to the top of the 180cm (6ft) fence, the long flower stems bore scented, pastel-coloured blooms which distracted the eye from the close-boarding behind. There is no reason why you should not use runner beans in a similar way. Their orange-red flowers are very decorative and the plants grow quickly to clothe their supports: the beans themselves are an extra bonus.

On a more esoteric note, the tender *Rhodochiton atrosanguineum* has flowers reminiscent of bougainvillea, in that the purple calyx is the showiest part of the blossom. Inside, the corolla forms a dark black-purple tube. The leaves are small and light green and reminiscent of ivy. I have seen this growing in a pot, where its vigour has obviously reduced, but in the open ground in a sheltered spot, it can make a substantial display; it will only be successful in the United States in regions where summers remain cool.

Climbers: particular virtues
Since most of us have small gardens, we have to be selective in the plants we choose to grow. Using the house walls and garden boundaries gives extra planting space, but this can almost make the problem worse: one's appetite is whetted for climbers, but many of them are totally unsuitable for a restricted area.

With their romping growth and attractive coral-red flowers, runner beans are worth growing as ornamentals but they are also valuable for their crop.

They may simply be too big. The Russian vine (*Polygonum baldschuanicum*; the very similar *P. aubertii* is more common in the United States), is a beautiful plant, whatever its detractors may say: those foamy inflorescences of cream flowers are so generously produced over such a long season that the whole plant becomes a soft, pale blanket, but the blanket is too large and all-enveloping to be laid over a little garden. As a veil to obscure some of the more brutal aspects of modern architecture, or to decorate the huge blank walls of a cinema, its prodigious vigour could be stretched to the full.

Other plants are less aggressive, but they are too dull. In a small garden you need well-mannered plants of moderate size, but the plants must also pay their rent: they must be pleasant to look at, if not positively stunning, for most of the year. A prima donna, which needs cosseting and tending, cannot be afforded in a prime position if it will only contribute to the garden picture for a brief spell. *Hydrangea petiolaris*, for instance, is a good plant for a north wall, and I am very fond of it, but honesty requires me to point out that it takes several years to become established, it is not evergreen and the large cream blooms fade to unprepossessing brown after a mere two or three weeks of glory.

The honeysuckles come high on the list of desirable climbers. They are

Among the hydrangeas there are several species that climb, attaching themselves to surfaces by means of aerial roots. The most commonly grown is *H. petiolaris*, a vigorous deciduous species that can clamber into trees as well as covering walls. The flower-heads, which develop in midsummer, consist of tiny fertile and larger sterile flowers. The rich brown stems are beautiful in winter.

Although the *Bougainvilleas* are unfortunately not suitable for growing outdoors in cool temperate climates, further south they can be grown as hedges or trained. Here, a vivid specimen climbs over an arch creating a brilliant display.

Top left: The honeysuckles are a large group of shrubs and climbers, including many that are worth a place in the garden. The American species *Lonicera sempervirens* has flowers of unusual colouring, but unfortunately neither these or those of its cultivars are scented.

Top right: Lonicera sempervirens 'Sulphurea' has clear yellow flowers which are often still in bloom as the showy fruits ripen.

Bottom: Lonicera tragophylla, a deciduous honeysuckle, has large but unscented flowers and thrives in shade.

hardy; they have conspicuous, usually scented flowers of fascinating construction; they often produce attractive fruit later in the year; they are easily trained and pruned. There are more than a dozen varieties to choose from, so try to see different kinds in the flesh, but the commonest – selected forms of the English wild woodbine, *Lonicera periclymenum* – are as good as the rest. Bees love the sweet trumpet flowers and their berries are clear, translucent red: attractive to birds, but not so much that they are immediately stripped and eaten. Like other woodland plants honeysuckles are usually happier with their roots shaded; on a hot wall they are more likely to become infested with aphids, so save the warmest aspect for plants that need its protection.

In the eastern United States, the Japanese honeysuckle has given the group a bad name for its rampant nature. The others, however, are well behaved. Good varieties include the goldflame honeysuckle (*L. x heckrottii*), and the trumpet honeysuckle (*L. sempervirens*). Both bloom from early summer until the frosts, and the latter produces translucent red berries.

For winter flowers, shrubs must be relied upon, but there is a clematis that blooms in winter and that you might try in just such a sheltered corner. *Clematis cirrhosa balearica* has divided, ferny leaves which assume bronze tints

Firm and reasonably durable supports are essential if climbers are to be seen at their best. This wall is equipped with galvanized wire strung between vine eyes, netting and trellis.

during the colder months. After a good summer the shoots will have ripened enough to produce buds and the small yellow flowers with their purple spotted interiors (and sweet scent), will open throughout winter, weather permitting.

How to support climbing plants

As we have seen, climbing plants do not all climb in the same way. Be sure to bear this in mind when deciding how to support them against a wall or fence. Even self-clingers will need initial propping; later, high winds may detach their extremities which will then need tying in to prevent the whole plant collapsing in subsequent

gales. And climbers which use tendrils or twining petioles need a support of small diameter so that they can cling properly – hefty trellis would be less useful than a system of wires.

Plant supports must first of all be strong. Most climbers are large, vigorous plants that are intended to be permanent features of the garden. Training and pruning to make them into things of beauty will take several years or more, so do not risk losing a fully developed climber by skimping the initial task of affixing suitable supports. As well as being strong and properly attached, your chosen supports should (rather like underwear), be as unobtrusive as possible; one's

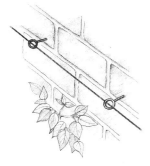

Galvanized wire running through vine eyes or screw hooks makes an ideal plant support.

Star jasmine (*Trachelospermum jasminoides*) and flanking roses have been planted in a narrow border beside the house and are being carefully trained on horizontal wires to frame the window.

attention should be drawn to the display not the underpinnings.

Old walls often bear the marks of nails and wire used by generations of gardeners, and one can add to these honourable scars as necessary. On a new wall, the counsel of perfection is to run strong galvanized wires (US size No 18) along its length at intervals of, say, 30cm (1ft), supported by vine eyes. These are special 15cm (6in) long screws with a loop at one end and they should be fixed in drilled holes with wall-plugs. Where vine eyes are unavailable, substitute galvanized screw hooks (US size 12 or larger) with the hooks bent closed. The advantage of vine eyes over other nails and screws is their length: the wires are held several centimetres away from the wall so that the climbers tied in to them have the benefit of better air circulation and are thus less susceptible to disease, there is also more space for plants such as clematis to wrap themselves around the wires. And if the entire wall is wired up you can move plants or alter the design at whim, knowing that the wires are already in place.

For some twining climbers, such as clematis or honeysuckle, 30cm (1ft) between horizontal wires is too far for the shoots to reach without flopping, but with garden string (of suitably subdued colouring), it is easy to make vertical supports just where you need them. In many cases, this kind of

climber looks better when grown over another plant (see Plant Combinations, p.83), but this is not always possible – an alternative is to attach a mesh to the wall for support.

'Clematis supports' – rolls of plastic-covered net available in various widths and shades of green or brown – are one such alternative. These are attached to a wall or fence with nails or screws at the corners, but although convenient, I do not like them because they remain far too visible and the plastic never weathers. Far better is ordinary pig-wire. Most people will be familiar with chicken wire – pig-wire is obviously stronger and is composed of large squares rather than small hexagons. It is galvanized to protect it from rust and its plain grey blends better with most walls than any kind of plastic.

Twining plants should be allowed to grow around and behind whatever support is provided – how could you stop them anyway? But this is not the case for other climbers, notably those with stiff branches. Such plants should be tied on to the wire, but I have often seen roses especially growing in horribly contorted shapes because a thoughtless gardener has poked the new growth through the mesh instead. As the shoots thicken they grow around the wires and become impossible to move, making pruning a nightmare; the only answer is to cut the rose to the ground and start again.

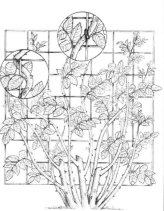

The details show (*left*) the wrong way of tying this rose to the trellis and (*right*) the correct method.

·CLIMBING ROSES·

There are a bewildering number of climbing roses and the beginner cannot be blamed for ducking out of the choice and opting for the first plant offered by the local garden centre. But because roses exist in such variety, you will discover (if you do not already know), that some are more to your taste than others and that certain roses, however much you may admire them, are simply too vigorous for a small garden.

It is helpful to look at each of the three main groups of climbing roses: the species, the ramblers and the true climbers. The species are the roses that occur naturally in the wild (one can stretch a point and include selected forms that have not been hybridized), such as the English dog rose, *Rosa canina*, or the American *R. virginiana*. These two are not climbers, but I use them as examples because most people will be familiar with them and can recognize their single flowers and decorative rose hips as distinctively 'wild'.

The climbing species, then, have similarly simple flowers and tend to share an equally short flowering season, but this is often compensated for by a later display of hips. The foliage and general form, too, retain their individuality. They have the toughness and disease resistance of wild plants but, unfortunately for those with small gardens, they also have untamed natural vigour.

But if you have the space to devote to a species climber, you will enjoy its spartan simplicity, so far removed from blowsy or dazzling examples of the rose breeder's art. *Rosa longicuspis*, for instance, has shiny dark green leaves that contrast well with the loose clusters of single white flowers. Later there is a good display of small orange-red hips, and in a mild winter the plant will keep most of its leaves. A less far-reaching plant that can be grown as a shrub or climber is *R. soulieana*, preferably in the selected form 'Wickwar'. The great beauty of this rose lies in its soft grey foliage. It too produces masses of single flowers (white, but decidedly cream in bud), and small orange hips, but it is the pale leaves that contribute most to a garden composition.

Rambler roses are also vigorous plants that flower only once a year and it is often said that they give of their best when allowed to sprawl rather than when trained against a wall or fence. This is largely true, especially

Climbing roses are the classic flowering plants for clothing walls and archways. Horizontal training, as here along the top of a wall and over a doorway, encourages them to flower freely. The bare base can be hidden by other tall-growing plants.

Right: 'Complicata' is a shrub rose with long arching stems which can be trained against a support. Here it makes a magnificent foreground planting to a wall-trained rambler.

Below: Four specimens of the climber 'New Dawn' have been trained over this hexagonal pergola. After its first main display this rose repeats sporadically throughout the summer.

Left: 'Constance Spry' is a vigorous modern shrub rose that lends itself to training as a climber. The sumptuous flowers are borne in midsummer only.

Below: Many of the ramblers show a strong family resemblance, with small white or creamy flowers borne in dense clusters with great profusion in midsummer. They have pliable stems and are easily trained over pergolas.

since ramblers do tend to suffer more from the ravages of mildew in a sheltered place, but what could replace the well-loved 'Albertine', so often seen in pride of place on a cottage wall? The untidy pink flowers of this favourite rose have been breathing their sweet scent along village streets for nearly 70 years: yes, mildew is a problem but it does not usually strike until after the flowers have faded and the plant is so vigorous that it does not weaken.

Other familiar ramblers include the sugary pink 'Dorothy Perkins' which has a usefully late season. I am not over fond, though, of its tight bunches of pompon flowers, the colour is, to my eye, hard and unattractive.

The true climbers are generally less vigorous than either the species or the ramblers and their habit of growth makes them more amenable to training against a wall or fence. Many flower more than once, if not exactly continuously, and they may be just what is needed in a small garden. There are some shockers amongst them, though, such as 'Danse du Feu', whose light red flowers I find an unsympathetic colour that becomes worse with time, fading to a sort of ashy grey. It is recommended for a north wall, but there are plenty of others which will grow in shade so you can safely ignore this one.

A good example of this category of climber is the rose 'Leverkusen', which is not common despite having been introduced more than 30 years ago. It has large yellow flowers that are double and slightly untidy in a most charming way. They are produced more or less continuously. The light green leaves are deeply serrated and very healthy and the plant deserves to be more widely used. ('Leverkusen' was bred by the German rose grower Kordes: when this name appears in brackets after the description of a rose in a catalogue it is fairly certain to be a good variety.)

The three types of climbing rose require slightly different regimes when it comes to pruning. The repeat-flowering varieties make buds throughout the summer on the current year's growth, so they can safely be pruned during the dormant season. The species and ramblers flower on the previous year's wood and if you prune them in winter you will certainly be removing shoots that will bear the next crop of flowers. It is probably best, then, to cut out flower-bearing wood immediately after the blooms have faded, together with some of the new shoots if the plants seems to be getting overcrowded. Tie the rest in as they grow: with vigorous varieties you will need to do this several times during the summer. The exceptions to this advice are the species roses whose fruits you want to enjoy in the autumn. Pruning must obviously be delayed, but remember to keep as much new wood as possible (subject of course to the constraints of the space available).

Dead-heading is a therapeutic task when one does not feel energetic enough for real gardening, but nevertheless wants to do something constructive, but it is not quite as simple as it sounds. In the first place, it may not be necessary. If you want rose hips in the autumn, for instance, or if your ramblers are summer pruned in any case, then dead-heading is either counter-productive or simply a waste of time. It is the repeat-flowering roses which benefit from having their spent blooms removed, but only if it is done properly. Snipping the neck of the flower will make the plant look neater but it will not in any way encourage the production of more flowers. Instead, you must cut further back, to

just above a likely looking bud from where a new rose should emerge.

Roses which make flowers throughout the summer are using a lot of energy to do so. It is particularly important to feed them properly, with a mulch of good manure every spring and perhaps some bonemeal as well. They need adequate supplies of water, too, so these are not the plants to try and grow in difficult situations where the soil is poor.

When choosing a rose, you should have a particular site in mind. This, of course, applies to the choice of any plant, but all too often one buys something on impulse at a nursery or garden centre without having the first clue about where to plant it. It is particularly important in this case to select site before plant because climbers are so visible, being both

Below: Although it is often badly affected by mildew, the rambler 'Dorothy Perkins', which flowers in late summer, has retained its popularity.

Right: The single-flowered 'Ballerina' is generally grown as a lax shrub about 120cm (4ft) high but it can be trained as a short climber.

large and raised above the general planting level.

Ask yourself first whether you do in fact want a rose. Roses come in all shapes and sizes but a different climber or even a shrub might be a better choice if the space to be filled is a tall narrow bit of wall, such as the area between two windows or next to a door. This is because roses flower much more freely if their shoots are trained horizontally; in a vertical space they will shoot upwards and produce flowers well above head level, leaving you to contemplate their spiny legs. It is of course possible to use a large climbing rose to clothe the face of a house, training it vertically at first and then spreading the shoots across above the windows; you will need a good ladder and a head for heights to keep such a plant under control. But gardening is not for the lazy in any case, and you may long to pick roses from your bedroom window and enjoy their scent on summer nights. Who am I to dissuade you?

Having decided that it is a rose you want, aspect is a constraining factor. A north wall is not impossible for roses; most catalogues include a short list of varieties that can manage without much sun and such a list could probably be extended considerably. Roses in general are not supposed to like shade, but I know at least one good garden where a fair number grow in the inhospitable shade beneath trees and they are all flourishing.

A south wall may in fact be more difficult because of the heat and lack of water. There are some slightly tender kinds (such as the old climbing tea roses or the yellow banksian roses) that need the protection of a south wall, but a hard winter may still cut them back or kill them, so in a small garden it might not be worth risking them. In southern regions of the United States the banksian roses (*R. banksiae*) are often grown for their evergreen foliage as well as for the small clustered flowers.

West and east walls pose no particular problems except where they may be exposed to high winds. Rose leaves can be battered and spoilt by a gale, just like those of any other plant, and extra care must be taken to tie in new growth regularly.

Having considered the practical problems of choosing a rose, there then comes the much more contentious issue of aesthetics. Although tastes vary widely, there are some points that should brook no argument. The colour of the wall or fence against which the rose will grow is of great importance. It goes without saying that a bright pink rose will not look its best in front of hard red brick, yet this mistake is often seen.

New red brick is a difficult background to cover, but you should be safe if you restrict your roses to shades of white, cream and yellow. Older, weathered brick is much more forgiving and silver pinks are possible. Against pale stone or a white painted wall or fence, the only restrictions are those imposed by the colours of the already established plants. A new wooden fence, treated but unpainted, seems as tricky as a new red wall, because its orange-brown colour is equally dominating. But since wood weathers faster than brick, fading over a couple of years to a soft grey, and because roses will take at least this long to become established, plants should be chosen to complement the eventual rather than the initial colour.

With well over 200 climbing roses available, it is possible only to scratch the surface when mentioning particular varieties, but I cannot leave the subject without listing some of my particular favourites.

If space is at a premium and a totally reliable, repeat-flowering rose is wanted, then 'New Dawn' is the answer. Its flowers are pale pink, of medium size and lovely shape, and the foliage is glossy and healthy. The main crop of blossom appears a little later than the main rose season and flowers continue to open sporadically throughout the summer. It is not particularly thorny, dead-heading it is a lovely chore because of its scent and it will grow on a north wall. A final bonus is that it is ridiculously easy to propagate by cuttings, so you can give its offspring as presents to deserving friends.

For those less keen on pink flowers, (I once heard it said that too many pink flowers gave a garden a boudoir air), there is the rose 'Mermaid'. This is a more vigorous plant and its almost evergreen foliage is its first asset: the leaves are distinctively large and glossy dark green. 'Mermaid' has single yellow flowers with darker stamens, each bloom measuring 7-10cm (3-4in) across, and they are produced throughout the summer, even on a north wall. They are scented, too. Peter Beales' rose catalogue concludes 'Mermaid's' description with the words 'Invaluable and unique'. I fully agree, but must warn newcomers to this rose that it is very thorny, so pruning is a slow and painful process. The other possible drawback is its slight tenderness: despite being suitable for a north wall, an unusually severe winter will cut it back or kill it outright. If you decide to try it, do give it a year or two to settle in before judging its performance; it is a slow starter.

Where there is a large expanse of possibly unsightly wall to cover, a good choice is one of the vigorous white-flowered ramblers that will give one marvellous display of blossom. The most famous is 'Kiftsgate', but this is an absolute giant and it would be

The lightly fragrant, silvery-pink flowers of 'New Dawn' are borne over a long season but it is the initial display that is fullest.

The marvellously strong pink of 'Zéphirine Drouhin' holds its own well against a magnificent blue large-flowered clematis.

better to choose, say, 'Bobbie James', 'Wedding Day' or 'Seagull', all of which have small single flowers borne in large clusters and which are not quite so rampant. 'Mme Alfred Carrière' also has white flowers (tinged with pink), but hers are double and globular and produced more or less continuously. This is a good rose for a north wall, if it can be given enough space – I have seen it reaching the second storey of a house. For a lower wall or fence, the thornless 'Zéphirine Drouhin' has one of the strongest scents of all, even though some might find the cerise pink of her flowers a little harsh (in hot climates it blooms only once). There is a pale pink version, 'Kathleen Harrop', with a similar scent and equally kind lack of thorns.

One could continue: 'Etoile de Hollande' is the best red rose, 'Gloire de Dijon' shows a marvellous combination of buff, apricot and yellow in its flat, quartered, scented flowers and looks lovely against warm-shaded stone. 'Pompon de Paris' has tiny delicate foliage and small, double, bright pink flowers: plant it where you can stop to admire its diminutive size.

Finally, a rose does not have to be a climber for it to be set by a wall. I have seen shrub roses of the hybrid musk family looking perfectly happy and extremely pretty trained against a low wall. 'Buff Beauty', for instance, can reach 180cm (6ft) or more with support and the hybrid musks' double flowering season and health and vigour make them good wall plants.

· SHRUBS ·

A wall or fence makes a good background for all manner of shrubs but, since space is always limited, we usually use it for those plants that actually need shelter. To this category of slightly tender plants should be added the shrubs that benefit aesthetically from being sited in front of a wall and those that contribute to the overall composition of the wall.

Earlier in the book (in the section on The Wall as Environment, p.33), I explained how plants can be encouraged to flower more freely by being placed where the sun's heat is concentrated by a wall, and how the riper growth that results is more able to withstand winter cold. If you live in a northern latitude, a wall can help bring into flower those plants that need no such encouragement farther south. This applies not only to summer-flowering shrubs; there are several shrubs that flower in winter provided they have adequate shelter, which will be discussed a little later on.

Shrubs that simply look better against support are those which have a diffuse habit of growth and can otherwise appear insignificant. I am thinking, for example, of *Buddleia alternifolia* with its long, slender, drooping branches, decorated with small purple flowers in early summer, or of *Colutea arborescens*, which bears yellow pea-flowers throughout the summer amongst delicate pinnate leaves.

Other plants that can simply look different (not necessarily better), grown on a wall are shrubs that can stand hard pruning into architectural shapes. Pyracanthas, with their agreeable dark foliage and tolerance of hard pruning, are often used in this way, trained into espaliers or buttresses that punctuate more informal planting. Doing this inevitably sacrifices most of the blossom and fruit which in another situation would be the chief reason to have a pyracantha. Yew is another plant that may be set by a wall simply as an architectural device and in this case there is nothing to be lost, apart from a few berries, by hard pruning it to the shape required.

Some shrubs may be perfectly stable and need no tying in. Others, especially those that are being trained into a specific shape, will need to be attached to the wall or fence. As with climbers, a firm, regular arrangement of nails and wire provides maximum flexibility without being obtrusive. In general, the shoots of shrubs are less pliant than those

The firethorns (*Pyracantha*) are easily trained and shaped but severe pruning will reduce the summer display of creamy flowers and, more importantly, of the berries that follow.

A sheltered corner against a high wall suits *Abutilon vitifolium*, a beautiful and free-flowering shrub but vulnerable in cold winters.

of climbers so you must tie them in when they are still young and sappy.

One other reason for planting shrubs against a wall is to provide eventual support for climbing plants. This is more fully discussed in a later section (see p.80), but for now it is sufficient to say that this is the way that most climbers grow in the wild, and that it is by combining plants that the most complex and satisfying garden effects are created.

Quick growers

Faced with a completely bare wall or fence and wondering where to start, it is a good idea to see what grows in nearby gardens. There is no need at all to use the same plants as your neighbour, but you will be saved expensive mistakes by picking up clues about the soil conditions and local climate. If

rhododendrons flourish, for instance, then it should be possible to grow other plants that prefer an acid soil, such as camellias.

The aspect will dictate the planting to a great extent, as will the size of the wall to be covered. Most people are understandably eager to establish plants as quickly as possible, and I have already described some of the annual climbers which are invaluable in this respect. Many permanent climbers are also quick off the mark, but this is not generally true of shrubs. Some, though, make respectable-sized plants within three or four years and if you have a sheltered wall and well-drained soil it is worth trying any of the shrubs described below.

The abutilons belong to the mallow family and most of them have the open silky flowers so characteristic of the group: imagine a shrubby holly-hock and you will not be far off. _Abutilon vitifolium_ has, as its name suggests, vine-shaped leaves with an attractive felty covering making them soft and grey. The clear mauve flowers open flat and are produced over a long period from midsummer. The form 'Tennant's White' is equally good. _A._ × _suntense_ 'Jermyns' has darker flowers and the leaves are less grey. These make such rapid growth that it is necessary to tie them carefully back to the wall to prevent them becoming top-heavy. A severe winter can kill them, so as a precaution take cuttings for possible replacements.

Abutilon megapotamicum, especially in its form 'Variegatum', lacks the simplicity of those described above: the mottled green and yellow leaves are decorated by flowers rather like pendulous lanterns. The red papery calyx is more prominent than the yellow petals and purple anthers which protrude below and the whole effect is bright and exotic. One usually sees this grown in a greenhouse, but it should be happy outside on a warm wall.

The Californian lilacs (_Ceanothus_), are invaluable shrubs because of the

The species and hybrids of _Ceanothus_ include some of the finest blue-flowered shrubs. There are evergreen and deciduous varieties.

colour of their flowers. They cover several shades of true blue, rare in the shrub world, and the flowers are so densely carried that the whole plant is transformed. I am particularly fond of *Ceanothus impressus*, perhaps because it was the first of the family to come to my attention. I will never forget stepping into a garden in Kent and finding a specimen in full bloom, a blue cloud settled comfortably by its sheltering wall. The leaves of *impressus* are small and deeply veined and the plant is evergreen. There are deciduous ceanothuses but, although they are on the whole hardier, I prefer the evergreen varieties. The hardiest of these is 'Autumnal Blue' which has deep blue flowers in late summer and autumn.

Piptanthus laburnifolius is not often seen, but I have grown it on an exposed south wall and it made rapid growth. Its common name of evergreen laburnum is a help when visualizing it: the leaves are trifoliate and dark, glossy green (as are the stems), and yellow pea-flowers appear in early summer. The flexible shoots can be tied back as they grow, thus keeping this plant quite close to the wall, which can be useful when there is only a narrow border below. A ceanothus, on the other hand, will always grow into a rounded shape even if it is partly restrained: this is its natural habit and its beauty will be destroyed if it is grown in too confined a space.

Slower shrubs

These are the plants whose beauty and stature will increase over the years, to your (or your successor's) continuing delight. Try not to be deterred from planting shrubs which grow relatively slowly by the ungenerous thought that you will soon be moving house anyway; there is pleasure in watching infant shrubs progress and you will be establishing a framework for future gardeners to build upon.

On a large, sheltered wall there is nothing to beat the giant *Magnolia grandiflora*, more tree than shrub, whose broad glossy leaves are evergreen and whose flowers are enormous creamy white structures almost a foot across. These nestle amongst the foliage, sending forth a rich heavy scent from late summer well into the autumn. To be certain of having flowers from a reasonably early age, choose one of the named clones which are propagated from cuttings and are known to be reliable in this respect. 'Exmouth' has leaves whose undersides are covered with rust-coloured felt; 'Goliath' has wholly green leaves which are generally shorter and broader than the type. In the United States 'Little Gem' is good – it has small leaves and flowers; the hardiest variety is 'Edith Bogue', but its growth is stiff and less compact.

If the wall at your disposal does not extend to two storeys or more, try one of the smaller magnolias, preferably a variety with down-turned flowers so that you can gaze upwards into the heart of the bloom. *M. sieboldii* and *M. wilsonii* are similar wide-spreading shrubs with cup-shaped pendant flowers decorated with crimson stamens, but *wilsonii* has a more definite flowering period (just before midsummer): *sieboldii's* flowers appear sporadically throughout the summer. *M. sieboldii* is best suited to the eastern United States. Magnolias are not plants to chop and prune carelessly. Their natural habit is attractive without intervention, so you should only plant one where there is sufficient space for it to spread.

Magnolia grandiflora should be given a sunny aspect (and shelter from the wind to protect its leaves), and the same applies to *M. sieboldii. M. wilsonii* is more of a woodland inhabitant and does better in half shade. All like good drainage but none will tolerate drought. Their ability to thrive on clay soils and in spite of atmospheric pollution means they are useful to Londoners and other city-dwellers.

Less aristocratic but more appropriate for those who have only small gardens are the Japanese quinces. The older generation of gardeners who have no time (and quite honestly no need), for Latin names know these familiar plants as japonica, which is far easier on the tongue than the correct name, *Chaenomeles.* Whatever we call them (and they used also to be

The Japanese quinces (*Chaenomeles*) are very hardy spring-flowering shrubs, with a colour range extending from white through pink to crimson.

called *Cydonia*), these are amongst the hardiest and most trouble-free plants one can imagine, with a long spring-flowering season and the bonus of attractive (and edible), fruits in autumn.

The varieties most often seen fall into the salmon range of pink, but there are better kinds. *Chaenomeles speciosa* 'Moerloosei' has both pink and white flowers on the same plant, which gives it a charming resemblance to apple blossom; 'Toyo-Nishiki' is an equivalent which is more widely available in the United States. 'Simonii' has rich red flowers with prominent yellow stamens; 'Hollandia' is very similar. These quinces are perfectly hardy without the shelter of a wall, but you will find them useful for the low spaces beneath windows on any aspect because they make such pleasant, well-behaved cushions of flower, leaves and fruit.

Camellias are evergreen, winter- and spring-flowering (they also flower in autumn in the United States) shrubs which are ideal for sheltered city gardens. They must have neutral or acid soil which is well drained but also adequately moist: on limy soil it is perfectly possible to grow them in large containers, as long as they are watered with rainwater, not tap water which tends to be limy. The flowers come in a rather bewildering range of colours and shapes, so make

a choice only after seeing as many as possible. The *williamsii* camellias are reckoned to be the best for general planting, because of their long flowering period and graceful habit: varieties of *Camellia japonica* in contrast tend to be spring-flowering and have broader, less elegant leaves. In the United States, the small-leaved sasanqua camellias are very important. They flower for long periods in autumn and early winter, but are unfortunately less happy in Britain because they need reliably hot summers, but are well worth trying against a hot south-facing wall.

Formal versus informal
Mention of 'formality' and 'straight lines' can be enough to make some gardeners switch off entirely, so wedded are they to the idea of a 'natural' garden. Others are so determined to

Camellias are magnificent evergreen flowering shrubs. They are impressive alone, but can combine well with other plants, such as ivies and hollies.

wield total control that every plant is pruned to within an inch of its life, lawn edges are razor sharp and bare earth abounds. There is, of course, a middle way. A coherent design and attention to detail (nothing sets a garden off so well as a neatly mown and edged lawn, for instance), should be the framework within which most plants can be free to show their individual shapes and characters.

You may think that your wall shrubs should all be allowed to grow untrammelled, or that to devote precious space to plants which need neither shelter nor support is a waste of time, but I hope to show you that the inclusion of at least some formally trained wall shrubs can lift your garden out of the ordinary.

The simplest additions are clipped evergreens planted at regular intervals to punctuate the arrangement of other plants. These can then be placed informally, having regard simply to colour and form: one's eye will be carried along by the rhythmic repetition of the background. Yew is the classic example, because it is so easily clipped into whatever shape you wish – perhaps columns or buttresses – and because it is so hardy and reliable. On a sheltered wall, bay (*Laurus nobilis*) could be used; the aromatic shapely leaves are good enough to look at as well as to eat. Also for mild areas is *Pittosporum tenuifolium*, which makes an altogether brighter

mass because its crinkled pale leaves reflect so much light.

An espalier is a pretty shape against a wall or fence and it does not have to be confined to fruit. *Pyracantha* is often trained in this way to make a dark architectural statement, but you must be prepared to do battle with its thorns on a regular basis if the shape is to be maintained. Tie in new shoots while they are still reasonably flexible and do not allow the plant to grow away from the wall.

Several plants, then, lend themselves to both formal and informal treatments. *Chaenomeles* is another which can either be allowed to make a spreading plant (as described earlier), or tied quite tightly against a support. As it is so hardy, it can be trained up a fence – I have seen it look pleasing on an unprepossessing chain-link fence where it reached over 2m (6ft) in height. As with *Pyracantha*, the trick is to tie it back while the shoots are sappy. In summer the new growth can safely be pruned back so that the flowers, which appear on older wood, will be clearly seen in the following spring.

If you use yew in a formal way, there will be a great benefit in winter: the repeated evergreen will continue to give form to the garden even though more ephemeral plants are absent and colours are mostly subdued. For the same reason, it is a good idea to include at least some evergreens amongst looser plantings. *Choisya ternata*, the Mexican orange blossom, does not strictly need the shelter of a wall, but since it will grow in shade (as well as sun), it can be a useful low mound to place against a north wall where its shiny compound leaves and clusters of white scented flowers will make a bright patch in late spring.

Shrubs for winter and spring

There is no need for a garden to be bare and cheerless through the darker months. A selection of evergreens or a single variety repeated will give the garden a solid framework all year round; it is also a good idea to have at least one shrub that flowers in winter, where the climate is mild enough.

Winter jasmine (*Jasminum nudiflorum*), is by no means a rarity, but I would hate to be without it. Nothing else I know can touch it for length of season and generosity of flowering, except for tropical monsters like the gaudy bougainvillea. The demure winter jasmine cannot fail to please, with its small starry yellow flowers set along dark green stems. It can come into flower as early as September in England and it will continue, checked only by the severest winter weather, right through to March. In colder areas, it flowers in warm spells during winter and spring. It is actually a sprawling shrub that can look better

allowed to form a dense mound or to cascade down a bank or retaining wall, but it can be trained vertically if this is done tactfully by separating the shoots and tying them individually rather than in ugly bunches. A north wall is perfectly adequate for this jasmine, but other aspects suit it too.

If it is scent you are after, the wintersweet (*Chimonanthus praecox*), is a temptation. Its strange almost translucent yellow flowers with their red centres spring directly from the twigs and they are indeed sweet, but the plant grows slowly (more rapidly in warmer American summers) and may take several years before it begins to flower. In the meantime it will be taking precious space on your best wall (it needs plenty of sunshine), and looking extremely plain throughout the summer. A frost to which the winter jasmine would respond simply by producing more flowers will entirely spoil the wintersweet's display, so be sure you have the space and the patience before planting this beguiling but recalcitrant shrub.

Forsythia, in the form commonly grown, is all very well for cutting and bringing into the house in generous sheaves, but the shrub itself has little to recommend it, being lumpy and rather coarse. It is the kind of plant to put at the far end of a large garden where its blossom can be shamelessly plundered and where it is out of sight

Carpenteria californica is a tender shrub which, except in mild areas, benefits from the protection of a south-facing wall. The evergreen foliage is attractive all the year round and the large white flowers are a spectacular bonus in summer. Here the plant is shown off well in a sheltered corner, growing against a brick wall further shielded by trellis.

The most commonly seen form of *Coronilla glauca* has pea-flowers of vivid yellow. It is quite common for plants to begin blooming in winter, although the main flowering season is spring. There can also be odd flowers right through to autumn.

for the rest of the year. But forsythia flowers are actually rather pretty and there is one variety which displays them well, because they are spread out rather than being bunched dazzlingly *en masse*. *Forsythia suspensa* 'Nymans' is an arching shrub that looks well against a wall. Its stems are bronzed and the large yellow flowers are set along them on slender stalks in a most delicate manner. After flowering, the stems that have borne flowers can be cut back to within a few buds.

A much smaller shrub for spring is *Coronilla glauca*, a member of the pea family. It needs a sheltered position to protect its evergreen blue-grey leaves, but where it is suited its yellow pea flowers will appear over a long period from early spring, and sometimes even before Christmas. I knew one particularly well placed example, beside a front door next to a gnarled rosemary bush: the rosemary's blue flowers toned with the glaucous foliage of the *Coronilla* and the yellow was in bright contrast. Both shrubs clearly enjoyed their south wall and usually came into bloom together.

Summer shrubs

There is no shortage of summer-flowering shrubs; what is perhaps more difficult is to choose the ones you have space for. On a south wall the myrtle (*Myrtus communis*) is excellent. It is such a well-formed plant with its small pointed evergreen leaves and mass of scented white flowers after midsummer. The foliage is aromatic and myrtle should be planted by a door or window, or close to a garden seat, so that the pungency released by the sun's warmth can be enjoyed. If space really is restricted then there is a smaller variety, *tarentina*, which has narrower leaves. It flowers just as profusely and produces white berries after a warm summer (the common myrtle's berries are purple black).

Carpenteria californica is a good shrub, although its flowering season (in July), is not as prolonged as some. I like its elongated light green leaves and the loose but regular mass it makes against a wall; the flowers are a spectacular bonus. These are white, opening flat and clearly similar to those of mock orange (to which *Carpenteria* is related), but they are raised out of the ordinary

The Moroccan *Cytisus battandieri* (growing against the wall) is an unusual broom which in early summer bears clusters of yellow flowers that have a rich pineapple scent.

by the large central mass of orange-yellow stamens. Like the myrtle, this plant needs a well-drained soil.

Plenty of shrubs like to bask, among them the brooms, and one member of this family is too lax a grower to make anything of itself without a warm wall for support. *Cytisus battandieri* may like to be baked, but it looks beautifully cool with its silky silvery leaves and pale yellow flowers: planted in the company of other shrubs and climbers in similarly refreshing shades of blue, silver and yellow it can be stunning on walls surrounding a swimming pool. This broom's flowers are uncharacteristically arranged in short loose spikes rather like those of a lupin and they have a most surprising scent of fresh pineapple.

On a colder, shadier wall one must look towards hardier shrubs. Hydrangeas are not all mop-headed and lumpy: some of the species have a great deal more character and are happy against a north or east wall. *Hydrangea villosa* has leaves with an almost furry texture and hint of purple in their colour. Its lace-cap flower-heads are a subdued lavender and they remain attractive even when they have faded. As long as it is not too dry at its roots, the plant will even grow in the shade of trees and it brings quiet distinction to a garden. Do not try to train it flat: this hydrangea must be allowed to spread its peeling, somewhat stout stems over several feet.

A similar-shaped plant is *Hydrangea quercifolia*, whose leaves (as the name

Although not suitable for strict training, *Hydrangea villosa* is a valuable shrub for the shady side of a wall. The pale lavender flower-heads are borne in late summer.

suggests), roughly resemble those of the oak – the American red oak rather than the English oak, which is to say the leaves are jagged rather than roundly lobed. Apart from their interesting shape, the leaves colour beautifully in autumn. The flowers are creamy white and held in large inflorescences so this is a shrub to lighten a shady border.

Alternatively, there are several cotoneasters that are happy out of direct sunlight: *Cotoneaster horizontalis* (the herringbone cotoneaster) has rather stiff branches, but when well trained becomes a striking waterfall of foliage and fruit. *C. franchetii* has an open habit of growth and its shoots are pliable and easily trained, so a wall or fence can be clothed with its soft sage-like foliage. In a mild winter, the leaves will be retained. Bees enjoy the small white flowers in summer and in autumn the plant bears red berries. Others that make excellent wall plants are *C. dammeri* and creeping forms of *C. salicifolius*. Both *dammeri* and *salicifolius* are especially attractive in winter with evergreen foliage.

Autumn shrubs

The transition from summer to autumn is a gradual one, but the flowering of certain plants always signals that the year has turned. The South African *Phygelius capensis* is one such indicator. Technically a sub-shrub which usually dies back to ground level over winter, it can remain evergreen in southern gardens against a warm wall and this will give it a head start over an open-grown specimen. Its leaves are an unremarkable dark green, but above them appear long shoots set sparsely with drooping tubular flowers in a warm shade of coral. The roots run mildly, so the plant will colonize as far as it is allowed to go and the graceful flowering stems will be decorative up to 180cm (6ft) or more from late summer until a hard frost kills them off. Since the plant spreads at the root, you can easily dig bits up to give away: do this in spring rather than autumn, when new shoots are appearing, so that the plant can start growing in its new home immediately.

I have discussed *Ceanothus*, but it is worth mentioning that some forms flower in autumn as well. 'Autumnal Blue' is an obvious choice, but 'A.T. Johnson', which flowers in spring, also gives a lesser autumn display, and 'Burkwoodii' and 'Gloire de Versailles' flower from summer on into the autumn.

Perhaps because blue flowers are comparatively rare, one tends to seize upon good ones, and the diminutive *Ceratostigma willmottianum* is certainly that. Bluer even than the bluest ceanothus, which all have a hint of purple about them, the small plumbago flowers with their white centres are set in

The tiered arrangement of its branches is a characteristic feature of *Viburnum plicatum tomentosum* 'Mariesii'. It can look very handsome with a wall as background but take care not to destroy its attractive shape by pruning and training.

clusters at the end of wiry shoots. In fact, even this plant is tainted a little with red: there is a pinkish honey-guideline running down each petal and the corolla tube and tips of the calyces are pink. Nevertheless, this is a good blue plant and I recommend it for planting in the shelter of a sunny wall for the sake of its late and prolonged season. The leaves turn red before falling. Since this ceratostigma will reach at most 60cm (2ft), you should find space for it.

Autumn is the season for berries and some of the prettiest are borne by

varieties of the guelder rose or European cranberry bush (*Viburnum opulus*). Gertrude Jekyll recommended planting the snowball bush (*Viburnum opulus* 'Sterile') against a north wall together with *Clematis montana* for a spectacular early summer combination of pale flowers in the shade, but it is difficult to understand why she chose this sterile form which by definition cannot bear fruit. The ordinary guelder rose, or the smaller variety 'Compactum' in a more restricted space, would also give white summer flowers (more attractive ones too, being more like a lacecap hydrangea than the heavy pompons of the snowball bush), but with the bonus of wonderful red translucent berries later. The variety 'Xanthocarpum' has yellow berries. The vaguely maple-shaped leaves of the guelder roses all turn attractive colours too. The American cranberry bush *V. trilobum* is similar but less subject to aphid attacks in spring. Neither is adapted to the deep southern states.

Pyracantha berries are less jewel-like but they make up for their lack of star quality by their extreme profusion.

As explained earlier, if you want this display of fruit the plant must be pruned as little as possible, so plan for its gradually increasing bulk at planting time. Colours range from yellow to orange-red and the habits of the individual cultivars vary from upright to spreading, so a good nurseryman should be consulted once you have a particular site in mind. Maximum hardiness also varies widely from variety to variety (zones 5-8, although most thrive in southern climates), so be sure the one you choose is fully hardy.

The pyracanthas are grown chiefly for their brilliant berries – a few varieties have yellow fruits but most are orange-scarlet – but the densely packed flower heads make an impressive display in early summer.

·PLANT COMBINATIONS·

The essence of gardening is, I think, the assembling of plants into pleasing combinations. It is not sufficient merely to have good plants and to tend them carefully; they must be arranged so that each bears some relationship to its neighbours, whether in harmony or contrast.

If this is true of gardening as a whole, then it is also true when one comes to consider the planting of boundary walls and fences. The vertical space at one's disposal is limited and plants grown here will be prominently displayed, so they must be chosen with care. There are further opportunities and challenges for those prepared to try and grow several layers of plants, arranging climbers on top of shrubs or other climbers. More plants can be fitted into the garden like this, but blending them into a harmonious whole is an art.

One of the best ways to learn how to combine plants is to visit as many good gardens as possible. There may be walls almost hidden behind exuberant tangles of vegetation, where cascades of flowers fall artlessly between sprays of attractive foliage, and so natural is the effect that the guiding hand of the gardener seems nowhere in evidence. But a beautiful combination of plants is rarely completely accidental and there are several points to bear in mind if you want to create a similarly generous display.

The problems are both practical and artistic. The importance of thorough ground preparation, enabling plants to combat the droughtiness that occurs at the base of a wall, has already been explained and where several climbers and shrubs are to be grown together this preparation must be done with extra care, incorporating as much moisture-retaining organic matter as possible. Several plants together will be both heavier and offer more resistance to the wind, so whatever support system is used must be especially strongly attached to the wall.

Other practical considerations are concerned with the nature of the individual plants. Vigour is of prime importance: some climbers are so robust that they would simply strangle anything beneath them. Russian vine, Virginia creeper and *Clematis montana* all fall into this category. They should be used alone except if you have a large or remote area to cover, when you can risk planting two thugs and letting them fight it out.

A combination of catmint (*Nepeta*) and roses makes a conventional but attractive foreground planting to a wall-trained fruit tree.

Pruning requirements are also important. It is a general rule that clematis that flower after midsummer do so on shoots produced in the current year: they can safely be cut right back to within 30cm (1ft) of the ground each spring and they are thus ideal for training through a shrub because they never become too heavy and tangled. This is not to say that one cannot use those varieties that do not like such drastic pruning, just that tact and patience will be needed to keep them reasonably kempt and the host plant in good shape.

There is also the question of docility, which relates especially to plants armed with thorns. Some roses are no trouble at all and can be pruned and trained with little personal injury, but others are viciously armed – the much-loved 'Albertine' is unfortunately guilty in this respect. Pruning is difficult because the thorns hold the stems together and if other shrubs or climbers are involved then a major battle ensues.

A beginner feeling nervous at the thought of dealing with ever-worsening tangles of vegetation should start with a simple combination, such as a shrub needing little pruning with a climber that is cut back close to the ground each spring. An example might be a spring-flowering ceanothus together with a late summer clematis. The shrub has to be given a head start and

Several large-flowered clematis hybrids, including 'Nelly Moser', start to bloom in late spring when wisteria and some of the evergreen ceanothus are at their peak.

Among the best clematis to combine with roses are the cultivars of *C. viticella*, such as the carmine-red 'Ville de Lyon' and the deep purple 'Royal Velours'.

allowed to make a firm framework before it is asked to play host to the more precocious plant, but a ceanothus will have attained a sufficient size in a matter of three years. With this and other fast-growing shrubs, it is important to tie back the new shoots as soon as possible and to remove any branches that grow resolutely away from the wall or the whole plant will become unstable and bulge alarmingly.

Having planted *Ceanothus impressus* (let us say), and trained it carefully for two or three years, the time will have come to add the climber. Even though the intention is for the clematis to grow over and through the shrub, do not make the mistake of planting it too close to the base of the ceanothus or it will find the competition from the established root system too fierce. Dig a generous hole 45cm (18in) away and add the usual organic matter before carefully planting the clematis (rather deeply, see p.45). The fast-growing stems can be led towards the shrub with twigs and they will soon grasp it with their twining petioles. Take the trouble regularly to spread the clematis shoots and encourage them to grow all over their support, because left to themselves the stems will clump together and race to the top.

Which clematis is, as always, a matter for the individual, but against the small leaves of *Ceanothus impressus* I like to see the elegant small flowers of *Clematis viticella*, especially those of the variety 'Alba Luxurians', which are white with a hint of green. For a more sombre effect with the dark green background, try 'Rubra', whose flowers are a rich deep crimson. Alternatively, varieties of *Clematis texensis* have suitably small flowers, bell-shaped rather than flattened, and can also be hard pruned in spring. 'Etoile Rose' is cerise pink with bright silver margins, 'Gravetye Beauty' ruby red with brown stamens.

This example of a simple juxtaposition of shrub and easily-controlled climber could be multiplied many times and it is a useful formula for a small garden where you could not face more complicated maintenance. When looking for more ideas, try to see the plants in their entirety, not just in crude terms of flower colour. One summer I saw a combination that was ephemeral but surprisingly pretty: a Japanese quince untidy with new shoots, the translucent red of the freshly-opened leaves blending beautifully with the deep red of *Clematis* 'Gravetye Beauty' described above. These quince shoots had not been cut back in summer, and in this case the task had been delayed to great effect – a good example of a confident gardener bending the rules.

For gardeners with more space and plenty of enthusiasm, there is the further challenge of combining two or more climbers, with or without an underpinning shrub. Provided the plants share similar requirements in terms of aspect and soils, the sky is literally the limit here. Do not forget that the composition should be widened to embrace the plants in the border (if there is one), beneath.

Colour is of prime importance, not only of flowers but also of foliage, fruit and perhaps stems. Habit, leaf shape and the general scale of each plant are also factors that should be considered when assembling garden pictures. You may want to marry plants to give one knock-out display, but combining plants also gives the opportunity to extend the season of interest on a particular piece of wall by using plants with staggered flowering times or with other claims to attention such as berries or especially fine foliage. The best way to illustrate the possibilities is simply to give working examples. From these, you can choose which might be suitable for your garden and your capabilities: I hope too that you will then feel confident enough to work out ideas of your own.

One does not want to devote the whole or even a major part of one's garden to winter plants, but even so it is worth creating a pleasing arrangement for this season which, after all, lasts at least a quarter of the year. The best place to do so is on a north or east wall – any warmer aspects will be needed for summer plants – where

several evergreens will grow happily. Pyracantha, with its persistent berries, makes a long-lasting patch of colour and this can be combined with one of the many ivies. A particularly fine pairing is the yellow-berried *Pyracantha rogersiana* 'Flava' with the variegated Persian ivy (*Hedera colchica* 'Dentata Variegata'), which has large creamy yellow and light green leaves. More yellow and green can be added in the form of winter jasmine, the three plants together giving colour and interest from autumn right through to spring.

From the practical point of view, none of these plants is difficult to deal with. Depending on the degree of formality you want, the pyracantha can be trained against the wall or left to grow more naturally, and the ivy will eventually be self-supporting although it will have to be tied to the wall for the first two or three seasons. Winter jasmine should be tied to wires and the spent shoots (which have borne flowers), shortened in spring.

Combinations of foliage give good value since they are attractive throughout the summer and flowers are a welcome bonus. Although generally *Clematis montana* is not a fit companion for other plants because of its vigour, I have to admit that I have seen it looking superb with summer jasmine. The jasmine's delicate pinnate leaves echoed the pointed compound leaves of the clematis on a much smaller

Here a foreground of lady's mantle (*Alchemilla*) and day lilies (*Hemerocallis*) backed by tall feathery plants and a wall-trained rose make a coherent planting scheme.

scale and the tiny jasmine flowers were scattered over the mixed greenery. Early in the year, when its dense mass of bloom appears, the clematis will be the dominant partner, and it will be necessary to watch that it does not eventually take the upper hand. Both the clematis and the jasmine twine readily up wires or netting and neither will need pruning except to keep them within bounds.

It is fun to combine plants with even greater disparity in their leaf sizes: the great leathery hands of a fig tree with summer jasmine again, for instance. Where there is space to give them free rein, *Vitis coignetiae* can be planted with

Clematis orientalis for a spectacular autumn show. The vine's enormous leaves, up to 30cm (1ft) across, become brilliant red and make a fine background for the clematis's dangling yellow flowers which are like lanterns cut from lemon peel. Earlier in the year, there is simply the contrast between the big, plain vine leaves and the small, delicately divided clematis foliage; as winter approaches the clematis produces silky seed heads in great profusion. Here again, no special pruning is necessary but the vine will need a certain amount of tying in to support its considerable weight.

Turning more specifically to flowers,

Right: Wisterias are such vigorous climbers that they are not swamped by the double yellow banksian rose, itself vigorous but slightly tender.

Below left: Roses and honeysuckles are a simple but successful combination.

Below right: The potato vine (*Solanum jasminoides* 'Album') and a large-flowered clematis make an attractive background to border plants.

a very simple device to extend the season is to plant close together both the early and the late Dutch honeysuckles (*Lonicera periclymenum* 'Belgica' and 'Serotina'). In this way you will have flowers from late spring until the autumn, those of the later plant mingling with the translucent red berries of the earlier variety. I have found that these plants need little pruning, but shoots can be removed after flowering, leaving a couple of buds at the base of each.

Another idea is to combine plants that bear the same or similar coloured flowers, either concurrently or at different times. Against a stone wall, I have seen a venerable wisteria given a new lease of life as well as a second, vicarious, season by the addition of the clematis 'Perle d'Azur'. The clematis had been trained along the wisteria's gnarled horizontal stems and up into its foliage and the purple-blue flowers, together with a few late offerings from the wisteria, appeared from midsummer until October. Being a late-flowering clematis, 'Perle d'Azur' can be cut down in spring and the new shoots trained each year. But to expect it to make so much growth and give a good display from a standing start, especially in the face of competition from an older, larger plant is not realistic unless it is given a good mulch of farmyard manure every autumn and ideally some liquid feed during the summer.

'Perle d'Azur' is a favourite of mine, because of its clear blue-lavender flowers and long, reliable season. It is a good choice to combine with a rose, such as the blush pink 'New Dawn' (see the section on climbing roses), whose main flush of flower is over by the time the clematis gets going, but which still carries scattered blooms whose colour makes a pale contrast to the clematis's blue. Roses and clematis are, in general, good bedfellows since they share a taste for a good rich diet and a top dressing of rotted manure will suit them both. The colour range of clematis is more limited than that of the huge rose family, but overall the possible combinations are numerous indeed.

Maintenance problems are reduced if, as in all the examples so far, you choose a clematis that can be pruned hard. You can then take a good look at the rose in spring and remove any dead, diseased or crossing branches with the clematis well out of the way. The early clematis and the double-flowered varieties which only produce double flowers on older wood are really best grown over shrubs that need less attention.

Although they do not climb much above 2m (6ft) or so, the perennial peas are good plants to associate with some of the less vigorous roses. From a practical point of view they are extremely easy, because the aerial parts die back each winter and the rose beneath can be pruned without encumbrance: aesthetically, they are very pleasing as they resemble their close relatives, the sweet peas, with their distinctive long-stalked flowers. Unfortunately, they lack scent but their long season more than compensates. *Lathyrus latifolius* is a strong magenta pink that can be hard to blend with other colours, but there is a lovely white form, 'White Pearl', which is more useful, and there are pale pinks as well.

I have also seen a perennial pea trained through free-standing trellis together with the spring-flowering *Clematis macropetala*. The clematis's ferny light green leaves looked fresh after the slaty blue flowers were over and the pea provided colour later in the year.

A shady wall need not be devoted purely to winter plants. *Hydrangea paniculata* makes a spectacular show of its cream flowers for three weeks after midsummer and this pale theme could be taken up by others whose flowers show up particularly well out of the sun. The climbing rose 'Mme Alfred Carrière' carries pinky-white clusters of double flowers, globular in shape, more or less continuously throughout the summer and she is perfectly happy in the shade. This rose can climb to two storeys but you can confine her to a more restricted space if need be. Another pale climber suitable for a north wall is the clematis 'Marie Boissellot' (also known as 'Madame le Coultre'), whose broad white sepals overlap to make fat,

satisfying flowers. This variety is vigorous and free-flowering, and can either be cut back each spring or left alone. In company with other climbers, you will probably find it easiest to cut it back.

To end this section on combining plants, I will describe a corner of a garden that was devoted solely to plants with yellow foliage. The background was an old brick wall, some 3m (10ft) high with an arched gateway in it. To one side of the gate was a golden tree, *Robinia pseudoacacia* 'Frisia', which had been trained to echo the curve of the archway, and against the sunny wall were two yellow climbers: a golden hop (*Humulus lupulus aureus*) and the variety of ivy called 'Buttercup'. In the border below were groups of golden feverfew and the cheerful annual *Limnanthes douglasii*, otherwise known as the poached egg plant. Such uncompromising devotion to one colour would have been cloying in a larger space, but the effect here was to illuminate the gateway even on a cloudy day. Notice too the unusual use of a tree as a wall decoration, simply because it had the right coloured foliage. The yellow ivy is actually trickier to grow than most varieties, being a slow climber and difficult to establish, but it is a memorable plant. It needs sunshine and the best colour will be seen in spring: later growth can be light green.

These weathered walls and statuary are enhanced by a predominantly 'golden' planting scheme which includes the honeysuckle *Lonicera × tellmanniana* and the variegated leaves of a low-growing *Euonymus* (centre foreground). The *Parthenocissus henryana* clinging to the wall will contribute in the autumn when its leaves turn to a vivid flame-colour.

·FRUIT·

Growing fruit against a wall or fence combines beauty with utility. The trees or bushes can be trained against the vertical support into formal shapes that have the double advantage of fruiting heavily and looking very attractive. Warm walls offer a particularly benign environment where peaches, apricots, nectarines, and figs can be grown – especially in cool climates where they would not otherwise receive enough summer heat; but shadier aspects are useful too, supporting morello cherries or soft fruit such as gooseberries and redcurrants. There are few more satisfying sights than a group of well-trained fruit trees against a wall or fence, but there can be pitfalls and these must be considered in order to avoid expensive mistakes.

In the first place, the pruning must be done properly (see p.152 for advice). The principles behind the espalier, fan, or cordon are simple enough, but many people seem to be nervous about pruning and there is little room for error. A good specialist book will contain clear pictures and unambiguous instructions and, thus reassured, all one needs is patience and enough time to approach the task. Try also to visit a garden where there are

Opposite: Even a small garden can accommodate fruit trees grown in trained shapes such as this fan-trained morello cherry which is highly ornamental as well as productive.

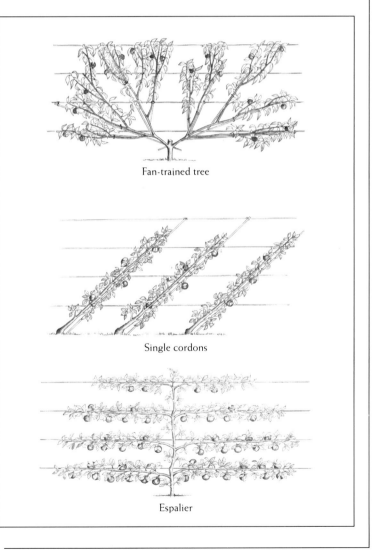

Fan-trained tree

Single cordons

Espalier

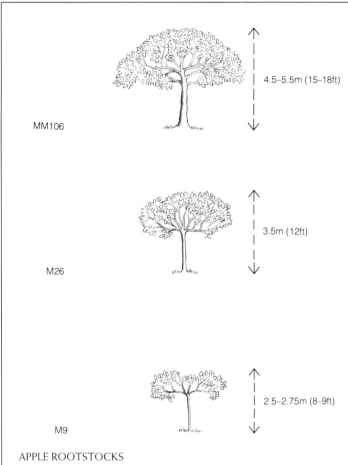

4.5–5.5m (15–18ft)

MM106

3.5m (12ft)

M26

2.5–2.75m (8–9ft)

M9

APPLE ROOTSTOCKS
The most useful rootstocks for apples grown against a wall are M9, M26 and MM106. MM106 is semi-dwarfing: for instance, cordons on this rootstock should be planted 60–90cm (2–3ft) apart and an espalier would spread over about 4.2m (14ft) of wall. M26 produces smaller trees: cordons should be spaced only 45–60cm (18–24in) apart and an espalier might reach only 2.5–3m (8–10ft). The M9 root system is correspondingly smaller and, given the possibility of drought at the foot of a wall, the better choice is M26, which will be able to grow further in search of moisture and nutrients.

good examples of trained fruit so that you can see what to aim for.

Fruit trees grown by a wall take up little ground space, but some of them need a lot of wall to spread over. The chief offenders are cherries, especially the sweet varieties (which must also be netted if birds are not to steal them), but pears and some apples can also make large plants. In a small garden trained fruit trees may be difficult to accommodate, stylistically as much as anything: it is hard to marry the strict formality of an espalier, say, with the loose forms of a buddleia or a rampant clematis. Where there is more space, a solution might be to confine the fruit either to the more formal area close to the house or else to use fruit trees together with whatever vegetables you choose to grow, to make a kitchen-garden in miniature.

Good nurseries will supply ready-pruned young trees and for the beginner these are to be recommended, as the framework is clearly delineated and there is a pattern to follow in subsequent years. However, these are relatively expensive, costing perhaps three times as much as a maiden or whip (unpruned, one-year-old tree), and they will only be available for selected varieties. The price is probably justified, bearing in mind the trained tree will be three years old, but if you want to grow an unusual variety then there may be no option but to train it yourself.

Apple and pear cordons are generally trained obliquely, to encourage fruit production, but the stems can also be grown vertically.

Vines are among the loveliest climbers but outdoor grapes need a sunny and sheltered position and careful pruning to produce worthwhile crops.

The points made earlier about improving the soil before planting close to a wall apply here too, with certain provisos which will be mentioned as appropriate. For support, a firm framework of wires held at least an 2.5cm (1in) away from the surface of the wall (to allow air circulation and reduce the risk of disease), is essential.

Apples and pears are usually trained into espaliers against a wall. This familiar pattern, in which tiers of branches are tied horizontally, is satisfyingly symmetrical and certainly more emphatic an outline than the other common alternative, the cordon. A cordon tree has only a single stem (although sometimes multiple cordons are seen), usually trained at an angle of 45° to restrict sap flow and increase fruit production. The great advantage of the cordon is its tiny demand for space, so that even in a small garden one can accommodate several varieties of fruit, but naturally such a small tree can give only a limited crop.

It is also possible to train apples and pears into a fan shape, but in general this is more suited to stone fruit such as plums, apricots and cherries which all fruit off new side-shoots. Exceptions are the so-called 'family trees' where three apple or pear varieties with similar vigour are grafted onto a single root and the resulting tree is trained into a fan. These are mentioned again below.

Almost all fruit trees available today are grafted onto special rootstocks (usually certified free from disease) chosen to reduce the vigour of the scion and make the tree easier to keep within bounds. When deciding which varieties to grow, it is important also to consider the rootstock or else the tree will be either too expansive or too small for the space available.

Pears are more deserving of warm wall space than most apples, because they need sun and shelter from wind: their blossom appears a fortnight before the apples', when frost is more of a risk and when pollinating insects are few; later in the year the relatively thin-skinned fruit are more easily damaged by heavy rain and wind. They are grafted onto Quince A or Provence rootstock which makes them much smaller than the wild pear but, since they root only shallowly, grafted pears need good soil rich in organic matter.

In order to set a good crop of fruit, the blossom of most fruit trees needs cross-pollinating. This simply means that (with a few exceptions), it is a waste of time to plant only one variety of a particular fruit. The problem is slightly complicated by the fact that not all apples, for instance, flower at the same time, but catalogues of good fruit nurseries are clearly marked with the flowering season of each variety so that it is quite easy to choose those which flower together. A few apple varieties are not reliable as pollinators and these too will be marked. With the 'family trees' mentioned above, pollination will take place between the different branches of the same tree.

Peaches, nectarines and apricots are all natives of China and thrive best in a continental climate that can offer a sunny spring, hot summer, dry autumn and sharp, well-defined winter cold. Britain, with its notoriously unpredictable weather, is not the best place to try and grow these trees: in early spring, conditions are often too poor to allow good pollination, but against a south wall there will at least be enough heat to ripen what fruit is set. A south wall should also be dry enough to keep the growth tough and hard: the peach family does not do well on rich living. In areas of high rainfall, it might even be beneficial to pave over the roots to prevent the trees growing too lush.

Cool moist climates are not ideal for peaches but a fan-trained tree grown against a warm wall can produce reasonable crops.

These fruit trees (peach, nectarine and apricot) are all self-fertile and so any one could be grown alone, but pollination by hand is recommended if the weather is chilly and damp when they are in flower, using a soft brush to transfer pollen from flower to flower.

Another fruit which does better under fairly harsh conditions is the fig. If its roots are allowed to spread freely the plant tends to make masses of foliage and bear very little fruit. Instructions are often given to box

the roots entirely, but it should be sufficient to put in a hard layer of stone a couple of feet below the surface or, as for peaches, to pave over the roots. In any case, figs only ripen after a hot summer in England, but in most of the United States they fruit readily where they are hardy. Their big leathery leaves are so attractive that I would not begrudge a plant space on a south wall. A fig can be trained very formally into a fan or left to grow into a more spreading bush, but this can quickly get out of hand and pruning then is tricky without spoiling the overall shape.

As mentioned above, fruit need not be restricted to south and west walls. The morello cherry is always in mind for a north wall and it does indeed thrive in the shade. There may not be space, though, in a small garden for this tree because, even on Colt dwarfing rootstock, it makes a wide-spreading (up to 3.5m/12ft) specimen.

Where there is limited space, consider growing red currants as cordons, or gooseberries trained into fans. Either of these would be very decorative against a smaller wall (about 120cm/4ft high) and the red currants can then be easily netted against birds. Gooseberry plants, with their sharp prickles, require careful handling when being pruned and trained, but once this is done the subsequent fruit picking will be much easier. Air circulation

Fruit trees grown as espaliers against a wall can very easily fit in at the back of a mixed border, giving form to the planting all the year round.

close to a wall is inevitably reduced, so it is sensible to choose varieties resistant to mildew.

Fruit trees that flower early should not be risked on an east wall, because of the danger of frost combined with morning sunshine (frozen petals warm too quickly and collapse), but late-flowering apples and pears are possible, as are the hardy plums 'Marjorie's Seedling' and 'Victoria'. Other plum and greengage varieties do better facing west. They are usually trained as fans (on St Julien A rootstock); the recently introduced Pixy rootstock reduces vigour even more and specimens grown on it can be trained as cordons.

Finally, do not forget vine fruit such as grapes and Chinese gooseberry (kiwi fruit). Ornamental vines were mentioned earlier in the book, but it is perfectly possible to grow grapes for eating as well as wine-making on a warm wall. A cordon vine takes up relatively little space and can be combined with fruit trees on the same stretch of wall.

The Chinese gooseberry (_Actinidia chinensis_), is related to the ornamental _A. kolomikta_. It is attractive too, with its broad heart-shaped leaves and reddish hairy shoots; the flowers are cream, darkening to yellow and the fruit appears in late summer. If there is space to accommodate both male and female plants (they are vigorous climbers and both are necessary for pollination) and a sunny wall sheltered from spring frosts, then these are certainly worth trying.

A pair of vines flanking a doorway shows how ornamental grapes can be, especially when varieties are chosen for the quality of their foliage.

·PLANTS FOR RETAINING WALLS·

Retaining walls offer a wide variety of growing environments and therefore the range of suitable plants is correspondingly wide. A wall of a certain aspect will naturally be appropriate for a particular category of plant, but even within the same stretch of wall there will be a moisture gradient, from dry at the top to damper at the bottom. Well-drained sites near the top of a sunny wall face are ideal for many alpine plants and shadier, cooler walls suit ferns, but there are many other plants which could be grown on the strength of their cascading habit.

After aspect and the acidity or alkalinity of the soil (pH), the height of the wall is the next thing to consider, because this will determine the scale of the planting. On some retaining walls there will be space to have both cascading plants and a layer of cushiony or spiky plants in a border at the wall's base, but more often one is restricted to planting the top of the wall together, perhaps, with any spaces in its face.

If you plan to grow plants in the wall face, the counsel of perfection is to set them as the wall is built, spreading the roots carefully and generally making them comfortable before continuing with the building. Often, though, one is faced with an existing dry-stone wall, possibly full of weeds such as couch, bindweed and ground elder that must be eradicated. Short of demolishing the wall, this means using chemicals: a translocated herbicide, such as glyphosate (sold under the names 'Roundup' and 'Tumbleweed'), applied to the weeds when they are in active growth, will kill them right back to the roots in a fortnight or so without harming the soil, although well-established weeds will need at least two applications.

When the wall is clean, it should be possible to remove a few stones without weakening the overall structure and attempt to establish selected plants in these spaces. This is difficult simply because in the first place it is hard to excavate a big enough hole and then to water effectively: most will just pour straight out again. The best chance of success is to grow plants from seed or cuttings in peat pots and then to insert the whole thing, pot and all, into the wall. The roots then suffer minimum disturbance and until the pot finally disintegrates it will hold the earth (and moisture) firmly around them.

Roots can be a problem in themselves, because some are so questing that in time they can seriously damage a wall. The most obvious culprit is valerian (*Centranthus ruber*), which seeds itself generously and has tall inflorescences of red, pink or white flowers above slightly glaucous foliage. It is a lovely thing, especially in the white form, and I am happy to have it in my garden, but the roots do need watching. If a wall does show signs of weakening and begins to crack, you should use a translocated herbicide to kill the plant; its roots penetrate so effectively that attempts to remove it physically would only damage the wall further.

Most people will be familiar with the bright spring combination of mauve aubrieta and acid yellow alyssum often seen cascading down rockeries or retaining walls. Unfortunately, this partnership has become rather a cliché, and also has the major disadvantage of extreme dullness for the rest of the year. Most alpine plants flower in spring and early summer, an adaptation to their natural habitat where the growing season is short, so it is always easier to clothe a sunny wall for the first half of the summer than to continue the display into the autumn.

Alpine enthusiasts will have no difficulty in filling all available crevices with choice specimens and the

Valerian (*Centranthus ruber*) and snow-in-summer (*Cerastium tomentosum*), both of which are established in this wall, are lovely plants but both need watching, the first because its penetrating roots can damage stonework and brickwork and the second because it will quickly smother less vigorous plants.

plantsman may be more interested in the individual treasures than the overall design, but for the 'ordinary' gardener (whoever that may be), the most important thing is that the retaining wall should look attractive for as long a season as possible. This means choosing reliable plants with staggered flowering seasons which also look presentable when not in bloom.

In certain situations, it might be best to use only one or two plants, for instance a mass of *Alchemilla mollis* at the damper foot of the wall, with mounds of lavender bulging over the stone at the top. Or perhaps white valerian as the sole occupant of a sturdy wall.

Such restrained planting is very restful and maintenance is simple, but the allure of other plants is strong and in a limited space one might find it difficult to adopt this purist approach.

A good nursery catalogue is useful in planning what to grow, but be aware that the word 'spreading' in a plant's description can be a euphemism for 'ineradicable weed'. The pretty snow-in-summer (*Cerastium tomentosum*), is a lovely thing with soft grey foliage and masses of bright white flowers, but it spreads by tenacious white roots and will smother anything in its path. *C. tomentosum columnae* gives the same effect but is altogether better

Pink, red and white forms of valerian (*Centranthus ruber*) top a retaining wall down which cascade streams of the alpine aster (*Aster alpinus*).

Dense planting, which includes a straying blue marguerite (*Felicia amelloides*), obscures the hard lines of a wall made of artificial stone.

mannered. Some of the dwarf campanulas are similarly greedy of space, although their roots are not quite so hard to remove, so choose varieties of *Campanula carpatica*, *cochlearifolia* or *turbinata* for their less aggressive habits.

The low-growing phloxes make good wall plants, either trailing over the edge or spreading over the wall face. *Phlox subulata* 'G. F. Wilson' has milky blue flowers in summer and should be lightly trimmed after flowering. The lovely *Phlox* 'Chattahoochee' is slightly more difficult to please: it needs cool soil which does not dry out, such as may be found near the foot of a retaining wall. As long as the site is rich in organic matter I would try this plant for its lax habit, dark narrow leaves and wide heads of silky blue flowers.

In contrast to these cool whites and blues, the rock roses (*Helianthemums*), provide the warmth of yellow, orange, pink and flame red in their fragile papery flowers. These dwarf shrubs can spread over as much as a square metre, so do not be fooled by their diminutive size in pots at a nursery. Several can be used together to spread and mingle, making an impressive display in early to midsummer.

For more ideas of what to grow, please refer to the plant dictionary at the end of the book (see p.131), but I will just mention one or two plants which are useful for prolonging the season. One that is attractive throughout the summer is *Geranium wallichianum* 'Buxton's Variety'; a marvellous, slightly trailing plant which produces white-eyed blue flowers over its divided foliage. It is sometimes difficult to obtain, but seed sown as soon as it ripens has given me plenty of new stock. These can easily be tucked between other plants and the stems will weave themselves gently into their neighbours, which could include *Oenothera missouriensis*, a prostrate evening primrose with bright yellow flowers over glossy foliage that likes good drainage. This gives colour for many weeks after midsummer. Most polygonums tend to be rampant, but *Polygonum affine* 'Superbum' reaches a height of only 23cm (9in) and does not spread uncontrollably. It carries short-stemmed spikes of pale pink flowers from midsummer through to autumn, when the spreading leaves (which persist throughout the winter), turn foxy brown. Less demanding of space is *P. capitatum*, which has more rounded flower heads and prettily marked leaves. Though not very hardy, it often behaves as an annual and reseeds itself prolifically.

Where there is space, try to include some small shrubs to give some form to all these herbaceous plants. Rosemary can make a plant of great character if it is allowed to sprawl from the top of the wall. The hardiest species is *Rosmarinus officinalis* but in a sheltered spot the mat-forming *R. lavandulaceus* would be worth a try, for its smaller, dark green leaves and bluer flowers.

Cytisus × kewensis is a prostrate broom which is covered in creamy flowers in early summer. After its season, though, it is rather dull, so this would be a good place to add the trailing geranium mentioned above, so that its blue flowers could decorate the plain foliage of the broom.

Shady retaining walls

A shady retaining wall is ideal for plants that do not like direct sunlight, although there might be problems with drought towards the top of the wall. Local conditions of soil and rainfall will determine if this is the case, but in general it is safest to set those plants that need damp soil towards the bottom. The drier but still shady parts will be suitable for some of the smaller varieties of ivy and certain sedums, including *S. sieboldii*.

There is not such a bias towards spring and early summer interest here, because many suitable plants, especially the ferns, are grown for the sake of their foliage. The maidenhair ferns are so delicately constructed that one is surprised to find that there are hardy varieties. *Adiantum pedatum* and *venustum* will both thrive in a sheltered damp position. In complete contrast are the broad, undivided leaves of the hart's tongue fern, *Asplenium scolopendrium*, which is such a good fresh green. A close relative *Asplenium trichomanes*, is a smaller plant with divided leaves and it has the advantage of surviving happily in drier conditions; it will be quite safe towards the top of the wall. *Blechnum penna marina* is a dwarf fern with divided evergreen fronds, but it is sensitive to high summer temperatures in the southern United States.

Flowers are possible too, of course. In spring, the lungworts flower for at least two months and there is no reason why they should not be tucked into a wall. *Pulmonaria saccharata* 'Highdown' has good rich blue flowers and these contrast well with those of *P. officinalis* 'Sissinghurst White'. There are pink and red kinds too, and several have attractively mottled leaves; these do become larger and rather coarse in summer so keep these lungworts for lower parts.

London Pride (*Saxifraga × urbium*), is usually seen as an edging plant but it too is happy in a wall. The rosettes of glossy leaves are always presentable and the airy, pale pink flowers are an early summer bonus.

Erinus alpinus is a compact plant with a spreading habit, covered in midsummer with purple or white flowers. It is usually recommended for a sunny position, but there is a shady wall near

A low retaining wall edges a small pool. The planting is suitable for a cool corner and includes a hosta, *Astrantia* and *Alchemilla mollis*.

Lavender, roses and other plants brimming with flowers top the wall beside this short flight of steps and are beautifully matched by pot-grown plants below.

the sea in Northern Ireland (it is hard to imagine a damper environment), where this plant has become naturalized over its entire face. The wall is more than 3.5m (12ft) high and I include this example just as a reminder that the rules of gardening are not absolute, and that a little experimentation can yield surprising and satisfying results.

More conventional shade plants include the violas, in all their marvellous variety. These are capable of flowering throughout the growing season, provided you dead-head them now and again, and offer some liquid feed two or three times a year. It is hard to beat *Viola cornuta*, in blue and white, but there are also a bewildering number of named hybrids. 'Hunterscombe Purple'

and 'Ardross Gem' I have found to be especially good doers.

The adaptable family of herbaceous geraniums includes species and varieties suitable for both sun and shade. On a tricky, dry shady wall I would certainly try *Geranium macrorrhizum* in either its white form or the magenta 'Bevan's Variety'. This makes comfortable-looking clumps of aromatic leaves which turn red in autumn. The flowers are not spectacular, but pleasing none the less over midsummer, and some of the foliage is retained through the winter. *Geranium endressii* 'Wargrave Pink' produces silvery pink flowers throughout the summer and its slightly shiny foliage would make a refreshing picture in a difficult corner.

• HEDGES •

Like a wall or fence, a hedge will constitute a fundamental part of a garden, acting as both barrier against the outside world and background for the planting within; in a larger garden, hedges can also make internal divisions. Wherever they are used these living barriers make excellent windbreaks and give added interest to the garden through the seasons; they can also be shaped or be of a colour to complement individual planting schemes.

Although a formal hedge might superficially resemble architecture, it has completely different qualities: it needs regular maintenance in the form of pruning and feeding, and its roots can extend far into the garden, depleting nearby soil of moisture and nutrients. And a high hedge will be broad at its base, taking far more ground space than either a wall or fence.

As a background to the rest of the garden, a formally-clipped green hedge is often the best option. Against such a hedge all kinds of colour schemes are possible and if it is evergreen there is the bonus of its quiet outline even in the winter. The tone of the green will depend not only on the exact hue of the leaves but also on their size and the degree to which they reflect light.

Of course there are exceptions to this plea for restraint. Even small gardens may have sufficient space for a low, flowering hedge and there is often a case for choosing different coloured foliage to accentuate a carefully planned planting scheme. A driveway could be cheered by planting a hedge of shrub roses or berry-bearing cotoneaster – an effect that might be too overpowering in the garden proper.

Formal hedges

Formal hedges are more commonly planted than the informal variety, probably because they take up less space and are less assertive, allowing one to enjoy the contents of a garden without being distracted by the boundary. They can also be decorated with simple topiary shapes or clipped to arch over gateways.

A formal hedge should be straight, well-furnished from top to bottom with foliage and trimmed with as much precision as is appropriate to the setting. Absolute regularity should be striven for, especially in a strictly formal garden, but a cottage hedge can be allowed more leeway.

Many hedges are doomed from the start never to reach this ideal, simply

There are several species of arbor vitae (*Thuja*) that can be trimmed to make dense formal hedges. In this garden the massive effect of the hedges has been lightened by setting against them roses trained over arches.

because they are composed of the wrong sort of plants. I am thinking particularly of privet (*Ligustrum* spp.), and some of the fast-growing conifers sold as screening plants such as Leyland cypress. Privet makes so much growth during a season that it needs clipping every fortnight or so if it is to remain kempt. Of the conifers I shall say little except that many of them are forest trees which can only be kept remotely within bounds by vigilant lopping and trimming: they will never make a hedge you can be comfortable with.

In complete contrast is the best hedge plant of all, English yew (*Taxus baccata*), which grows more sedately and looks well on only one clip a year. *T. media* 'Hicksii' is a hardier substitute in much of the United States. Most plants are flattered by the yew's narrow, dark green leaves and it can remain hale and hearty throughout several centuries. Naturally, even such a paragon has its drawbacks and the first is expense. Yew is always costly to buy, but one can minimize this by choosing smaller rather than larger plants, when various sizes are offered. Plants of only two or three years will adapt more readily to their new home and will begin growing while larger specimens are still becoming established. Yew is slow-growing, and when you consider that it is this quality that makes it so easy to maintain at maturity, it is churlish to expect it to shoot up immediately

Top: Box (*Buxus sempervirens*) is traditionally used for low hedges in formal gardens, in which it gives a year-round framework of dark green.

Bottom: Giant pinnacles of yew (*Taxus baccata*) dominate a large garden in which informal planting is combined with formal elements such as topiary in holly (*Ilex*).

just to satisfy impatience. In fact, yew is no slower than some others such as beech, for instance, and if it is planted properly in enriched soil then it can make 30cm (1ft) or so of growth each year. The yew's most serious drawback is that it is deadly poisonous to grazing animals and must not be used where livestock could reach it. Even withered clippings are toxic and remain palatable, so disposing of them must be done responsibly. Yew berries are poisonous too, and could be attractive to children, but these will only be produced by a very overgrown hedge, unclipped for a number of years.

Another excellent evergreen is holly. It is, like yew, easier to establish as small plants. English holly (*Ilex aquifolium*) will make a good background to bright flowers although its shiny leaves have a very different quality from the matt green of yew. American holly (*I. opaca*) has a duller leaf and is more common in the eastern United States where it is hardier and grows more vigorously. Holly hedges can be brightly exuberant too, because there are many variegated types whose leaves are patterned with yellow or cream.

Clipping once a year will be sufficient, but the prickly offcuts are tricky to collect without injury and the leaves shed throughout the year will blow about the garden and make weeding near by difficult without gloves. To minimize discomfort, choose varieties such as *I. aquifolium* 'J. C. van Tol' or *I. × altaclarensis* 'Camelliifolia', whose leaves are almost spineless.

Box (*Buxus sempervirens*), is an old favourite, long used for both large and small evergreen hedges. For a boundary hedge, 'Handsworthensis' is a good vigorous form which can reach 3m (10ft) if necessary.

A good deciduous hedge can be made of beech (*Fagus sylvatica*). It keeps its old leaves throughout the winter so the hedge is never bare, but I find the foxy colour rather aggressive and am always relieved to see the pale green, new leaves bursting from their buds in spring. Copper beech can look splendid in the right place, but the degree of redness of the leaves varies, so choose a good strong colour from a nursery. The best, most uniform copper beeches will have been grafted and so are much more expensive than the variable plants raised from seed. The new growth during the summer will carry on it a succession of fresh translucent red leaves. The copper and green varieties can be used together to make a random tapestry effect or 'marbled hedge'. Hornbeam (*Carpinus betulus*), is superficially similar, but its corrugated leaves are less shiny than those of beech and they are held less tenaciously through the winter. They tend also to be a duller brown then, so I find them more suited to the darkest days.

Very useful in a small garden is the 'fedge', the narrowest hedge of all. To make a fedge, you simply cover a fence with a self-clinging climber, such as ivy. This gives the illusion of a hedge and should be clipped as if it were one, but it takes up much less space. The fence should be firmly constructed, but it need not be solid, because eventually it will be completely hidden. Since ivy, like holly, can be obtained in so many variegated guises, a fedge can be as restrained or as cheerful as you choose; the ability of ivy to thrive in dry shade means that even a dark corner can be brightened.

Informal hedges

The plants of which an informal hedge is composed are not clipped severely, rather they are allowed to express their natural habits and exuberance and are usually expected to produce flowers and sometimes berries as well. There is practically no limit to the plants that can be used in this way, so one can be as creative as one wishes.

But it is futile to plant an informal hedge unless there really is room for it to grow freely. The exact width depends upon the eventual spread of the plants used; this could be, as in the case of large shrub roses, several metres. However, if there is the space, an informal hedge has panache and proves the point that plants often look better when massed. Although difficult to plant against, the informal hedge is effective when dividing an expanse of lawn, say, or even screening a tennis court or other structure.

Many informal hedges do need some kind of pruning each year, either to keep them within bounds or to encourage flowering, and this may require more concentration and thought than simply clipping a formal hedge. Within the huge realm of roses, for example, the Japanese rugosas are undoubtedly some of the easiest to deal with as they need practically no pruning at all, whereas the shrubby hybrid musks are very much improved (and later flowering encouraged), by judicious dead-heading.

Roses do make some of the most sumptuous hedges and the range of sizes is so wide that there are varieties to suit a small garden as well as a long sweeping drive. The rugosas are good value not only because of their ease of maintenance, but also on account of their attractive papery flowers, decorative rose hips and healthy, disease-resistant, ridged foliage which colours well in autumn. In a smaller space, and in poor, sandy soils, the suckering Scotch rose (*Rosa pimpinellifolia*), and varieties thereof make a low dense hedge covered with small but abundant flowers in summer and blackish rosehips later.

Good hedge plants for mild areas are the hardier fuchsias which are free-flowering and have a naturally graceful habit. More lumpy and stolid, but in flower almost non-stop through the summer, are the shrubby potentillas, available in various colours ranging from white through pink and yellows to red. Lavender is often used as a low hedge, especially in the dwarf variety 'Hidcote'; this has an almost formal quality, because of its uniform growth and upright flower stalks. On a large scale, *Buddleia* can be grown as a hedge. Cut it back as usual in spring and in late summer it will attract great numbers of butterflies to further decorate the garden. Do not forget, either, the hawthorn, usually kept strictly as a formal hedge, but which can grow into a marvellous billowing mass, clotted with flowers in early summer and burnished with haws and glowing foliage in autumn.

Soft fruit bushes, such as gooseberries or red, black or white currants are the ideal size for a low dividing hedge within a garden. Their flowers are insignificant, but the fruit is very decorative (until you pick it), and the fact that you need to prune them to encourage generous production means that the hedge is kept neat.

Establishing a hedge

A boundary hedge should be sited so that at maturity it lies entirely within your property, enabling you to clip the far side (and collect the trimmings),

Top: A medley of pink and near-white roses makes an informal hedge that contrasts with a trimmed hedge of copper beech (*Fagus sylvatica* 'Cuprea'.

without trespassing on your neighbour's garden. In practice, the hedges between small gardens are often shared, so do discuss this possibility before planting a new hedge; the person next door might be glad to share the maintenance and possibly even the cost and work of planting, but if not, then you must stick to the letter of the law.

The establishment of a hedge requires proper ground preparation and absolute accuracy when placing the plants; skimping the former means the hedge will grow only slowly, whilst deviations from the proper alignment or spacing will be glaringly obvious, even to a casual glance.

PREPARING THE GROUND

Well before the hedge is due to be set, the earth must be thoroughly cultivated, ideally to a width of 90-120cm (3-4ft). The roots of most hedge plants will spread at least that wide in the first few years and preparing the soil around the initial planting trench will encourage them to make even faster growth. Digging should be thorough, and every scrap of weed root must be removed, because perennial weeds are very difficult to extricate from an established hedge. In most cases (except perhaps on light soils) it is important to dig two spits (a spit is a spade-depth), deep in order to loosen the soil and to break up any hard pan below the surface which would impede drainage. You should aim to incorporate a good deal of organic matter, say a wheelbarrow-full per couple of metres (yards) of the hedge's length, together with a 15cm (6in) potful of bonemeal.

Digging work is traditionally carried out in the autumn. The ideal is to have all the digging and soil improvement finished at least a few weeks before the hedge is to be planted, to let the soil settle. Broadly speaking, planting time depends on the type of hedging, but the prevailing weather will influence exactly when you set the plants; nothing should be done when the ground is frozen, and driving rain will lead to hasty work and horrible compaction of heavy soil.

PLANTING

Deciduous plants, such as beech, hawthorn and hornbeam are dormant through the winter and bare-rooted stock can be set any time after the leaves have fallen (or turned brown, in the case of beech and hornbeam). Evergreens, such as yew, holly and box, are slightly more difficult, because they never become completely dormant. They must be transported with earth around their roots, either wrapped in burlap or in polythene containers and they should be planted in autumn or spring. Autumn is probably the better season, as the soil keeps much of its warmth well into November and the roots will immediately grow to anchor and feed the plants. The soil in spring is cold and if you wait for it to warm up you run the risk of drought as summer approaches. However, for evergreen plants in areas which have severe winters, there is a greater chance of success if you plant in spring (as long as the plants are watered during the following summer), because young evergreen foliage is particularly susceptible to frost damage. In the end, the decision about when to plant must rest on knowledge of your local climate.

Make sure that the plants do not dry out during the planting; keep them in a shady place with their roots damp and take one plant out at a time. Stretch a line along the middle of the

PLANTING
When the weather allows, dig a trench in the middle of the cultivated strip, keeping it straight by using a line of string between two pegs. The trench should be 15cm (6in) deeper than the plants' roots and wide enough to allow them to be spread comfortably with space at both sides.

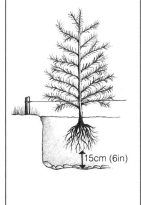

15cm (6in)

trench and see that it stays taut. Position each plant against the line at the same depth in the soil as it was at the nursery or in its container. Because the trench is deeper than the roots, some back-filling will be necessary — this will vary with each plant. After planting the soil should be firmed by treading and then the surface loosened with a fork.

Planting distances are debatable. A great deal depends on the eventual height one wants, as taller plants will need correspondingly more ground space. For a tall hedge, up to 180cm (6ft) or more, do not plant closer than 60cm (2ft) apart; with densely branched evergreen plants such as yew it is quite possible to increase this to 90cm (3ft). Wide spacing works less well with deciduous species, because the hedge can look gappy in winter. For smaller hedges, up to 120cm (4ft), 45cm (18in) is ample; dwarf hedges of box need the closest spacing: only 23cm (9in). Informal hedges have the widest spacing of all, since each plant is expected to grow almost naturally. They can be set just close enough so that they will overlap a little at maturity.

The easiest way to keep the spacing even is to cut a stick of the required length and hold it between adjacent plants. (Details of planting distances for different hedging plants are given in the Plant Reference section, p.138.) One single row of plants is usually perfectly adequate; there is no need to stagger them and make a double row.

Caring for a new hedge
However carefully planted, a hedge still needs consistent aftercare if it is to grow well. Unless rain is forecast soon after the planting has been completed you should water the new hedge immediately. Lack of water during the first growing season, especially after spring planting, will lead to losses, so during a dry spell you should be prepared to give a thorough soaking every fortnight or so. The best way to do this is with a perforated hose, which should be left on overnight. A foliar feed can also be beneficial, encouraging the roots to grow and seek the water that is available. A mulch of organic matter such as rotted leaf mould or grass clippings will help retain moisture.

During the first winter, a newly-planted hedge is vulnerable to both wind and frost. If the hedge is in an exposed position, especially if it is evergreen, it will benefit from some kind of shelter. Plastic netting specially developed as wind protection is commercially available and should be attached to firm posts on the windward side of the hedge. Even hedges in relatively sheltered sites can suffer in unusually high winds; if plants seem loose, retread the soil around their stems. Frost is capable of heaving soil

Right: Arches and windows in hedges reinforce their architectural character. On the initial stages of training some kind of framework is necessary to hold in place the growths that are to form the crossing section. Low hedges of box (*Buxus sempervirens*) can be seen between the walls of yew (*Taxus baccata*).

and disturbing newly-set plants, so again make a habit of inspecting and treading in any loose ones after a cold spell.

FEEDING

The organic matter and bonemeal incorporated at planting time will offer sufficient nourishment during the first year; thereafter, I like to apply a mulch of rotted manure in early spring, covering it with a layer of inert material (leaf mould, shredded bark etc), which will largely prevent the germination of the weed seeds invariably present in manure. If you live in a town and manure is scarce and expensive, use a balanced compound fertilizer to feed the hedge. Feeding late in the season is counter-productive, because it encourages a lot of sappy growth which cannot ripen and harden in time for winter; severe weather will cut this right back. Once the hedge has reached the desired height, feeding can be reduced, but it is important not to stop completely or the hedge will suffer. Remember that the plants are growing in unnatural proximity to one another, with fierce competition for root space, and that they are continually trying to compensate for the growth we remove by clipping.

PRUNING

Many deciduous shrubs have a naturally bushy habit and form branches close to

Naturally bushy plants should be pruned lightly after planting. Cut back the main stem and laterals by about one-third, making the upper shoots shorter than those lower down, the first stage of a batter.

the ground without hard pruning. Beech and hornbeam, as well as many evergreens such as holly and Portuguese laurel (*Prunus lusitanica*), are good examples. With these, it is sufficient simply to cut back the main stem and laterals by about one-third after planting. Be careful to cut the upper shoots shorter than those lower down: this is the first stage in creating the sloping face or batter of a hedge (the importance of which is explained below). Coniferous hedges such as yew and *Thuja* should be treated similarly except that the leader is not pruned.

You may have to harden your heart over pruning certain plants, such as hawthorn, blackthorn (*Prunus spinosa*), and myrobalan plum (*P. cerasifera*); these will never make a good bushy hedge unless they are cut right back after planting. Having toiled and sweated over correct planting, it is extremely difficult to bring oneself to prune every plant to a mere 15cm (6in), but this must be done. The reward will come during the following growing season, when there will be a satisfying proliferation of fast-growing side shoots right from ground level. During the summer a light trim all over encourages further side shoots. The hedge should be given another hard pruning the following winter,

Top: A formal hedge needs to be kept well trimmed. Yew (*Taxus baccata*) needs only one clipping a year, which should be done after midsummer. In general hedges should be cut with sloping not vertical sides.

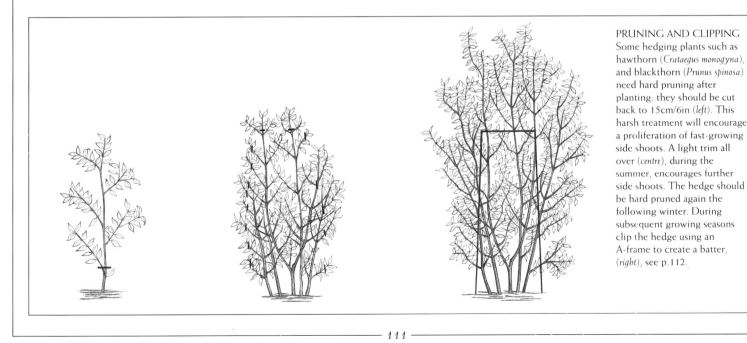

PRUNING AND CLIPPING
Some hedging plants such as hawthorn (*Crataegus monogyna*), and blackthorn (*Prunus spinosa*) need hard pruning after planting: they should be cut back to 15cm/6in (*left*). This harsh treatment will encourage a proliferation of fast-growing side shoots. A light trim all over (*centre*), during the summer, encourages further side shoots. The hedge should be hard pruned again the following winter. During subsequent growing seasons clip the hedge using an A-frame to create a batter, (*right*), see p.112.

when the main shoots can be reduced by one half.

CLIPPING

During subsequent growing seasons, the sides should be clipped, and the top reduced as well (except in the case of conifers, whose vertical shoots should only be cut once the hedge has reached its required height). The sides should not be absolutely vertical, rather they should be tapered from a narrow top to a slightly wider base. This batter serves two main purposes: it allows light to reach the base of the hedge and thus keep the lower leaves healthy, and (in evergreen hedges especially), the shape prevents a heavy snowfall or severe winds opening up the top and destroying the outline. In order to keep the batter even, you will need a template in the form of an

Yew (*Taxus baccata*) is extremely long lived and in time can lose its original shape. However, it is remarkably responsive to dramatic renovation provided that it is well watered and fed after being cut back.

A-frame which can straddle the hedge or else a specially made adjustable jig whose angle can be varied to suit each individual hedge. This can also be less precisely accomplished by running a second line along the bottom of the hedge. The top of the hedge can be kept level by clipping to a line of string stretched between two posts.

Once the hedge has reached its proper size, the frequency of clipping depends upon the type of plant and the finish you prefer. Yew looks perfectly acceptable on a single trim after midsummer, but will need two cuts a year if you want a sharper outline. Box hedging is usually intended to look very formal, so will need a trim every month. Beech and hornbeam need only one clip, probably in late summer. Clipping should be done before autumn, to allow the new shoots to harden off before winter. Trimmings can be composted, or burnt if they are too woody; remember the danger to stock from yew leaves, so never leave these lying around.

The plants used for informal hedges are treated in the same way as if they were grown as specimens. At planting, any damaged shoots should be removed, as well as any that cross each other. The aim should be to allow the plants to attain their natural habit, although any damaged, diseased or dead shoots must be removed each year. Other than this routine attention, many informal hedging plants, including _Berberis_, _Escallonia_ and _Potentilla_ need little or no pruning. See the Pruning section for details, p.149.

Renovation

Faced with a neglected hedge that has become lumpy and out of control, there may be a great temptation to grub the whole lot out and start again. Before writing it off as a hopeless case, though, it is worth trying drastic renovation. Starting with one side, cut the overgrown hedge right back to the main stems, in late spring for evergreens and during the dormant season for deciduous shrubs. This will look horrible but, given a good feed of manure and plenty of water, many hedges make a remarkable recovery and the shorn side will show new shoots during the following summer: it should be fully clothed with green after two or three years. If the treatment is clearly beginning to work, then attack the opposite side the following year.

· PLANT REFERENCE ·

● Shade	◐ Semi–shade	○ Sun

This Plant Reference section cannot be encyclopaedic, but I have tried to make as broad a collection of plants as possible.

Hardiness zones for each plant are based on the USDA hardiness zones of typical minimum winter temperatures (°F):
1 below -50, **2** -50 to -40, **3** -40 to -30, **4** -30 to -20, **5** -20 to -10, **6** -10 to 0, **7** 0 – 10 **8** 10 – 20, **9** 20 – 30, **10** 30 – 40.
The smaller zone number indicates the approximate northern limit of cold tolerance; the larger number indicates the estimated southern limit where this plant can be expected to perform. Sometimes heat tolerance plays as important a role as lack of winter cold in determining the southern limit. There will always be exceptions to these ratings since regional differences in climate such as hot or cool summers, humidity and snow cover can extend or limit a plant's range. Local microclimate also plays an important role with such factors as warm south-facing slopes, the amount of sun or shade, and wind.

In the eastern and mid-western United States plants may not survive in as warm a hardiness zone as on the Pacific Coast where summers are cooler. At the southern limit, these plants may not be as long-lived as farther north due to the lack of winter cold to force dormancy.

CLIMBERS

The heights given can only be approximate, based on good growing conditions: many plants may not reach the height given and some may exceed it, so use the figures to compare the relative vigour of plants, rather than as absolutes. Most of the plants listed here are woody perennials which make permanent features; a few are herbaceous perennials, dying to the ground each year, and some are annuals, growing from seed and dying in the course of a single summer. I have indicated where a plant falls into either of the last two categories. Each plant's method of climbing is also given. Where no special cultural needs are specified, the plant will thrive in ordinary well-prepared garden soil.

Aconitum volubile ◐○
(CLIMBING MONKSHOOD)
Up to 2m (6ft) · Herbaceous perennial · Twiner · Late summer · Zones 5–8

Unusual climbing perennial, useful for training through shrubs whose foliage will make a background in late summer for its hooded lilac-mauve flowers. Sun or part shade, in a moisture-retentive soil.

Actinidia kolomikta ◐○
4.5m (15ft), wide-spreading · Twiner · Foliage plant · Zones 4–8

The heart-shaped leaves of this large climber are most striking: purple-tinted when young, later becoming green, many of them with terminal halves coloured white and pink. There are insignificant white flowers in June. Colours develop best in full sun. Its close relative, *A. chinensis* (Chinese gooseberry) is described in the Fruit section.

Akebia quinata (FIVE-LEAF AKEBIA) ◐○
9m (30ft) · Twiner · Late spring · Semi-evergreen · Zones 4–9

This is a delicate looking plant with its compound foliage and graceful twining habit. The flowers are small, but they are an unusual maroon colour and sweetly scented. After a good summer, dark fleshy seed pods are produced. Despite being semi-evergreen, it is not a really good coverer, unless it becomes rampant in a warm climate. Plant in sun if you want the seeds, otherwise it will withstand partial shade.

Aristolochia macrophylla, syn. *A. durior*
(DUTCHMAN'S PIPE) ◐○
9m (30ft) · Spreading · Twiner · Summer · Zones 4–8

Vigorous twining plant with big, matt green, heart-shaped leaves, making a dense cover. Odd yellow green flowers (which inspired the common name) in June. Needs space. In the northern US it dies to the ground each winter, but is rapidly replaced by vigorous shoots each spring.

Campsis radicans (TRUMPET VINE) ○
9m (30ft) · Scrambler/self-clinger · Late summer · Zones 4–9

Exotic-looking climber needing a warm wall

and initial support although it is eventually self-clinging. Clusters of large tubular, wide-lipped orange-red flowers of velvety texture are freely produced on new wood, so prune hard in spring. The form 'Yellow Trumpet' has similarly rich colouring. *C.* × *tagliabuana* 'Madame Galen' is a less vigorous hybrid (reaching 7.5m/25ft) with larger flowers.

Celastrus orbiculatus ◑○
(ORIENTAL BITTERSWEET)
7.5m (25ft) · Twiner · Autumn colour and fruit · Zones 5–8

Vigorous climber perhaps at its best scrambling over an unattractive building, but worth the space for its yellow autumn foliage and jewel-like red seeds showing through split orange seed capsules. Choose a hermaphrodite plant which can produce fruit on its own.

C. scandens ◑○
(AMERICAN BITTERSWEET)
7.5m (25ft) · Zones 3–8

Less rampant than *C.orbiculatus* with larger, longer-lasting fruit.

CLEMATIS ◑○

Large family of mainly climbing plants (although there are herbaceous and non-climbing members), including many good species as well as large-flowered hybrids. The climbers use twining petioles; the most vigorous are capable of clothing a wall or fence alone, but most look best when grown through a shrub or a more substantial climber. There are varieties for sun as well as shade, but all like cool roots shaded from direct sunlight. Pruning principles are explained fully in a later section (see p.146).

The species
C. alpina
2m (6ft) · Spring · Zones 5–9

Pretty scrambling climber for spring, when the drooping violet-blue flowers open on old wood amongst divided leaves. 'Frances Rivis' is a good variety, with larger flowers and generally greater vigour. 'White Moth' has double grey-white flowers which resemble those of *C. macropetala* (under which name it is often listed). Any aspect.

C. armandii
3.5m (12ft) · Spring · Evergreen · Zones 7–9

This vigorous plant needs a warm wall to protect its leathery leaves and masses of early, cream flowers. The variety 'Apple Blossom' has pink tinges and bronze young leaves; 'Snowdrift' has pure white, somewhat larger flowers.

C. campaniflora
3m (10ft) · Late summer · Zones 6–9

Individual flowers on this spreading climber are small, but they are so generously and evenly produced that the plant is decorated over a long season with delicate, pale blue bells. Grows in sun or shade, and can be pruned hard in spring or else left to spread.

C. cirrhosa balearica
2.5m (8ft) · Winter · Evergreen · Zones 8–9

Only worth growing in a sheltered site, but a lovely climber to cheer the winter with its pale yellow scented flowers. Its ferny foliage is sparse, so try to grow it through a shrub.

C. flammula
3m (10ft) · Late summer · Zones 6–9

A delicate tangle of pale green leaves and a foam of small cream flowers produced from late summer into autumn. Good for trellis since it can be hard pruned each spring. Alternatively, let it grow up through a yew hedge for maximum contrast: dark solidity with pale airiness. Needs some sun.

C. × jackmanii
3m (10ft) · Summer (early summer in US) – autumn · Zones 3–8

Bears a closer resemblance to the large-flowered hybrids than to most of the species, with its large, velvety purple flowers. The variety 'Superba' has even larger blooms. Despite its frequent appearance clumped around a front door, not to be despised; it has a long season and is very hardy and reliable; the colour is true and strong. Any aspect.

C. × jouiniana 'Praecox'
3m (10ft) · Non-twining · Late summer · Zones 4–9

In Britain, be sure to obtain the variety 'Praecox'; the type species comes into flower so late that its display is inevitably cut short by the onset of winter, but in a warmer climate, it is useful for its late bloom. This will not cling of its own accord so must be tied to or draped over its support, but the vigorous stems can be trained against a wall with little difficulty. The divided foliage is dark green and the small flowers, white with purple shading, appear in profusion. Needs some sun.

C. macropetala
2.5m (8ft) · Spring · Zones 5–9

Rather resembles *C. alpina* in its unaggressive habit of growth and early flowering season, but its violet-purple blossoms are double, with a more dishevelled but none the less attractive air. 'Markham's Pink' has reddish-pink flowers, while the variety 'Maidwell Hall' has both pale and dark blue sepals. All produce attractive silky seedheads later in the year. Any aspect.

C. maximowicziana
9m (30ft) · Late summer · Zones 5–9

Vigorous, almost rampant climber common in gardens in the eastern US. Masses of small, fragrant white flowers in August-September. Maintain control through hard pruning in early spring. Similar, but stronger and hardier than *C. flammula*.

C. montana
9m (30ft) · Early summer · Zones 4–9

The most vigorous form of this free-growing climber is white-flowered 'Grandiflora', but any of them could clothe the front of the average house within five years or so, so plant only where there is space enough. They are all enchanting in May and June when covered with flower, and even young plants perform well. Consider planting two different varieties together so the flowers can mingle. The species has white flowers; those of 'Elizabeth' are soft pink, while 'Tetrarose' has distinctly bronzy foliage and large lilac-pink flowers. *Wilsonii* has smaller white flowers, but these prolong the season as they appear at the end of June, and they are also scented. Any aspect.

C. orientalis
7.5m (25ft) · Late summer · Zones 5–9

Otherwise known as the orange peel clematis, this has unusual yellow flowers with fleshy sepals that really do remind one of citrus skin. The leaves are ferny and the flowers are followed by silvery mop-heads of seeds. Needs some sun.

C. rehderiana
3m (10ft) · Late summer · Zones 6–9

The small tubular flowers with their recurving yellow petals are rather insignificant so plant where it can be seen in detail; sweet cowslip scent. Needs some sun.

C. tangutica
3.5m (12ft) · Late summer-autumn · Zones 5–9

Very similar to *C. orientalis* but generally less vigorous. Set above a large retaining wall, it can emerge through the stonework lower down and make a pretty mass with its lacy foliage and yellow lantern flowers; silvery seed-heads. 'Bill Mackenzie' is a particularly good form. Needs some sun.

C. texensis
3m (10ft) · Late summer-autumn · Zones 5–9

The hybrids of this species have small nodding flowers held on long stems. 'Etoile Rose' has cerise flowers with pink margins; 'Gravetye Beauty' ruby-red with brown stamens. All are useful for growing through earlier-flowering shrubs, because they should be pruned right back each spring. Needs some sun.

C. viticella
4.5m (15ft) · Late summer · Zones 4–9

Like *C. texensis, viticella* and its hybrids are ideal for growing through a shrub, perhaps the stiff stems of a viburnum or a rose. 'Alba Luxurians' is particularly unusual, with white, green-tipped petals; 'Rubra' is much stronger-looking, with deep crimson flowers. 'Purpurea Plena Elegans' has fully double, violet purple flowers that look like tight rosettes. Needs some sun.

Large-flowered clematis

A good clematis nursery will stock getting on for 100 varieties of large-flowered clematis, and breeders are continually seeking different colours and shapes. The types listed below constitute a personal selection of those I particularly like or which have been proved to be especially reliable. They should be suitable for zones 4 or 5 to 9.

THE WHITES

'Duchess of Edinburgh'
2–2.5m (6–8ft) · Early summer and early autumn

Usefully small clematis with double, white rosette flowers decorated with yellow stamens appearing early in the year on old wood; in September, single flowers are produced on the current season's shoots. Any aspect. No pruning.

'Henryi'
3.5m (12ft) · Midsummer-early autumn

Large creamy flowers with dark stamens. Any aspect. Pruning is optional.

'Huldine'
6m (20ft) · Late summer–autumn

The most vigorous white clematis; its flowers are relatively small, but very shapely (they do not open quite flat), with greenish stamens and mauve bars on the reverse of the sepals. Any aspect except north. Prune hard in spring.

'Marie Boisselot'
6m (20ft) · Midsummer–early autumn

Almost as vigorous as 'Huldine' with a long season, from June to September, but of different character: its flowers are larger and the sepals overlap to give a more solid appearance. Any aspect. Pruning is optional.

'Wada's Primrose'
Up to 2.5m (8ft) · Early summer and early autumn

More yellow than white but with a cool appearance: the flowers are cream with deep cream bars and yellow stamens. Ideal for a north wall, and does not need too much space. Do not try on a hot aspect. No pruning.

THE PINKS AND REDS

'Comtesse de Bouchaud'
2–2.5m (6–8ft) · Early summer

Produces masses of mauve-pink flowers and will grow on any aspect. Prune hard in spring.

'Ernest Markham'
Up to 3.5m (12ft) · Late summer

Deep red flowers with yellow stamens. Does best on a sunny wall. Prune hard in spring (but it will flower on old wood if left unpruned).

'Hagley Hybrid'
Up to 3.5m (12ft) · Midsummer–early autumn

Similar colouring and overall size to 'Comtesse de Bouchaud', but distinguished by pointed sepals and brown, rather than cream stamens; a more restrained grower. Needs some sun; good plant with a long season. Pruning is optional.

'Joan Picton'
Up to 2.5m (8ft) · Early summer and autumn

Small variety which will grow an any aspect. Rosy-lilac flowers with white bars and brown stamens – an unusual combination. No pruning.

'Mme Julia Correvon'
Up to 4.5m (15ft) · Early summer to autumn

One of the longest blooming varieties, except where summers are extremely hot. A bright clear crimson. Like other viticella hybrids prune hard in spring.

THE PURPLES AND BLUES

'Perle d'Azur'
Up to 4.5m (15ft) · Midsummer–autumn

A favourite because of its relatively good blue (not sky blue, unfortunately, whatever the nurserymen optimistically say), set off by green stamens, and because of its long season and general reliability. It should be hard pruned in spring so it never gets out of control. Any aspect.

'The President'
Up to 2.5m (8ft) · Midsummer–early autumn

Absolutely reliable variety. Large, slightly cupped purple flowers are held almost horizontally so that the greyer undersides can be seen. Flowers first on old wood and continues the display on new growth in early autumn. No pruning. Any aspect.

'William Kennett'
Up to 3.5m (12ft) · Midsummer–early autumn

Deep lavender with dark stamens. Less vigorous than 'Perle d'Azur' and slightly less free-flowering, but handsome none the less. Pruning is optional. Any aspect.

Cobaea scandens ◐○
(CUP AND SAUCER PLANT)
6m (20ft) · Subtropical vine · Tendrils · Summer–autumn · Zones 8–10

Commonly grown as a climbing annual, this is a good plant for instant cover in a sunny spot. The purple bell-shaped corolla springs from the green calyx in a fair approximation of a cup and saucer: the form 'Alba' has creamy flowers. Sow inside in early spring and harden off gradually, then train up strings until it can self-adhere.

Euonymus fortunei ●◐○
(WINTERCREEPER)
Up to 12m (40ft) · Spreader/self-clinger · Foliage · Evergreen · Zones 4–9

Often used as ground cover but when allowed to attach itself to a wall or fence it will climb to lofty heights. Relatively slow-growing, so also suitable for a smaller space. Fruit in autumn resembles *Celastrus scandens*, but smaller. Many varieties including striking variegated forms. 'Emerald Charm' has deep green leaves with conspicuous cream veins, whilst 'Coloratus' has shiny green leaves which take on purplish tints in winter. Sun or shade.

Hedera (THE IVIES) ●◑○
Foliage · Self-clingers · Evergreen

The ivy family has three main decorative species, all of which have variegated or otherwise distinctive cultivars. They are all evergreen and attach themselves to their support by means of aerial roots. Their beauty and variety are sometimes scorned, perhaps because they are such undemanding plants, thriving in most soils, on most aspects and withstanding atmospheric pollution. Although many are vigorous climbers at maturity, they may take several seasons before they become truly self-clinging, so support should be given. The aerial roots could damage an unsound wall, but there is no reason why ivies should not be grown on a strong surface; indeed, there is some evidence that ivy offers a degree of protection to walls by keeping them dry.

H. canariensis (ALGERIAN IVY)
4.5m (15ft) · Zones 8–10

Large glossy leaves on often wine-coloured stems give a lush appearance. Thrives in sun, so give it a warm wall which will also protect it in a hard winter. 'Gloire de Marengo' is a variegated form: grey green with irregularly cream-margined leaves.

H. colchica (PERSIAN IVY)
4.5m (15ft) · Zones 6–10

Large, leathery green leaves without the red stems of the plant above. *H. colchica* and its varieties are hardier than the Algerian ivy. 'Dentata Variegata' (zone 7) has large leaves with exuberantly irregular creamy yellow margins – an eye-catching plant. 'Sulphur Heart'

has a similar pattern in reverse, with a yellow splash in the centre of each leaf. Try either of these with the yellow variegated climbing jasmine (described below), for dramatic contrast in leaf size.

H. helix (COMMON IVY)
Variable height · Zones 5–10

There are well over 100 named forms of this highly variable plant, ranging from miniatures, such as 'Emerald Globe' which might decorate a small retaining wall to vigorous kinds, such as 'Cathedral Wall', which could cover the front of a house. The shapes of the leaves vary from almost rounded, such as 'Green Heart', to very pointed, such as 'Pedata', the bird's foot ivy, as well as several crinkled and wavy-edged kinds. Cream and yellow variegation is common, usually affecting the margins of leaves, but sometimes, as in the distinctive 'Goldheart', the leaf centres. The overall effect depends on the degree of definition or blending of the colours – some patterns are bold while others are subtle. Hardiness varies somewhat; some of the hardiest varieties are 'Buttercup' (with golden foliage), 'Galaxy', 'Harrison', 'Lustrous Carpet' and 'Tomboy'.

Humulus lupulus (HOP) ○
6m (20ft) · Herbaceous perennial · Twiner · Foliage · Zones 3–8

Vigorous plant grown commercially for the sake of its female flowers – the resinous papery hops that give beer its distinctive flavour. The large, three-lobed leaves are roughly toothed and very handsome, and the hops (borne only on female plants), are pale green in late summer and can be cut for drying. In gardens, the form usually grown is the

golden-leaved 'Aureus', which is almost as vigorous and a wonderful colour. Best in full sun, if possible with shade at the roots.

Hydrangea petiolaris ◑○
(CLIMBING HYDRANGEA)
15m (50ft) · Self-clinger · Early-midsummer · Zones 4–9

Gives excellent cover to a large wall once it is established: like the ivies, it takes a few seasons to begin to climb and spread – one can help it by watering well during its early years. Stems are held 30–45cm (12–18in) away from the wall, so do not try this where space is limited. Good for a north wall, but will also grow in sun. The roughly heart-shaped leaves are a refreshing shade of green and for a fortnight in June the cream inflorescences light up the whole plant. The rough, warm brown stems are pleasant in winter. Since the flowering season is so short, try to grow another climber in the same place; the white noisette rose 'Mme Alfred Carrière' looks lovely, as would a white clematis such as 'Henryi'.

Ipomoea tricolor (MORNING GLORY) ○
2.5m (8ft) · Annual · Twiner · Zones 8–10

This plant's sky-blue flowers are absolutely lovely, and in most of North America it thrives in the warm continental summers. 'Heavenly Blue' is one of the most popular varieties.

Jasminum officinale ○
(SUMMER JASMINE)
4.5m (15ft) · Twiner · Summer · Zones 7–10

The scent is heady and evocative, enjoyable from midsummer almost until autumn as clusters of white tubular flowers appear in succession to decorate the dark foliage. The foliage itself is almost reason enough to grow this plant – the leaves are matt green and delicately pinnate, and the twining stems are green too. It needs a warm wall and not too rich a soil to produce a good crop of flowers. The variety *affine* has larger, pink-tinged flowers. 'Aureum' has leaves blotched with strong yellow and needs siting with care – see above under *Hedera colchica*.

Lathyrus (PERENNIAL PEA) ○
3m (10ft) · Herbaceous perennial · Tendrils · Summer

The perennial peas are old garden plants which look best if grown through other climbers or shrubs. *L. grandiflorus* (zone 5) has magenta flowers, whilst *L. latifolius* (zone 3) has desirable white forms such as 'White Pearl'. *L. rotundifolius* has smaller flowers of an unusual soft brick colour. None of these species is scented, but all have a long season and they are easy to grow in a sunny place.

Lathyrus odoratus (SWEET PEA) ○
2–2.5m (6–8ft) · Annual · Tendrils

There are a great many named varieties encompassing a wide range of mainly pastel colours. The degree of scentedness varies. Use them to hide a fence or to decorate a trellis. Best grown in climates with cool summers; where summers are hot start early for spring bloom. Choose a sunny position and enrich the soil with good compost or manure.

Lonicera (HONEYSUCKLE) ◐○
The honeysuckles are twining plants of hedgerow and woodland, where they generally grow with their roots in the shade and their flowers reaching towards the light. Most are happy on a north wall.

L. caprifolium
3.5m (12ft) · Summer · Zones 6–9

Common cottage plant with glaucous perfoliate leaves; scented cream flowers appear at midsummer, followed by translucent orange-red berries. Little training or pruning is required; once the plant has grown into its support it should be allowed to hang forward in a sweetly scented tangle. If old or weak growth needs removing, do this soon after the flowers have faded and cut back to a point where new shoots appear.

L. × *beckrottii* (GOLDFLAME HONEYSUCKLE)
6m (20ft) · Late spring to early summer · Zones 4–9

One of the most vigorous and popular of the vining honeysuckles flowering continuously throughout the summer. Carmine-pink buds open to cream; new growth is reddish.

L. japonica
4.5m (15ft) · Summer-autumn · Semi-evergreen · Zones 4–9

The flowers are small, but they are produced continuously from midsummer and have a rich, sweet scent. Each flower opens white but turns yellow with age. This honeysuckle can be a vicious, rampant pest from the mid-Atlantic states south, so needs to be controlled in the garden. The form 'Aureoreticulata' is less rampant and usually grown for its foliage: it can be a shy flowerer, but its leaves are very bright – fresh green netted with yellow. 'Halliana' is the best variety if you want flowers.

L. periclymenum
2.5m (8ft) · Summer · Zones 5–9

There are various named forms of this, the European woodbine: all have richly scented flowers and decorative berries. 'Belgica' and 'Serotina' are the so-called early and late Dutch honeysuckles, which can be planted together for a prolonged display of cream and red flowers.

L. sempervirens
3.5m (12ft) · Spring-autumn · Semi-evergreen · Zones 4–9

Warm, orange-red tubular flowers which contrast well with the good green leaves. 'Sulphurea' has clear yellow flowers.

L. tragophylla
4.5m (15ft) · Summer · Zones 8–10

Vigorous species with very large, bright yellow flowers – most eye-catching – but unfortunately unscented. Likes its roots to be shaded, so try on a north wall or on sunnier aspects if other plants can supply shade.

Parthenocissus henryana ◐○ (SILVER VEIN CREEPER)
6m (20ft) · Self-clinger · Foliage · Zones 6–9

Grow this in the shade for the sake of its prettily-tinted leaves, similar in shape to *P. quinquefolia*. They are dark green with silvery veins and in autumn they turn bright red.

P. quinquefolia ◐○ (VIRGINIA CREEPER)
7.5m (25ft) · Self-clinger · Foliage · Zones 3–9

Large, vigorous climber, well capable of covering a house. Its foliage has a certain grace and movement, each leaf being divided into five leaflets; in autumn the matt green becomes fiery red and orange. Do not grow this on a red brick wall. Tends to be rampant in its native eastern North America.

P. tricuspidata (BOSTON IVY) ◐○
9m (30ft) · Self-clinger · Foliage · Zones 4–9

Often mistakenly called Virginia creeper. Its leaves are rather like ivy, varying between ovate and trifoliate, depending on age, and in autumn vivid shades of yellow and red are produced. Not a plant for a small garden, but useful to cover a large expanse of house wall or to hide an essential but unattractive building such as a garage.

Passiflora caerulea ○
(PASSION–FLOWER)
6m (20ft) · Tendrils · Summer · Zones 8–10

One needs a warm wall to grow the tender passion-flower with its intricate blue blooms and orange fruit. As it climbs by means of tendrils it needs frequent training to prevent its forming a tangle; the lobed leaves are decorative even if the flowers are sparse. 'Constance Elliott' has cream flowers.

Pileostegia viburnoides ●◐
4.5m (15ft) · Self-clinger · Late summer · Evergreen · Zones 8–9

A subtle rather than a startling plant, but good evergreen cover for a shady wall with its dark, leathery leaves and foamy cream flowers in late summer.

Polygonum aubertii ◐○
(CHINESE FLEECE OR SILVER LACE VINE)
12m (40ft) · Twiner · Late summer · Zones 7–9

A favourite of mine, but a plant to use with discretion as it is an extremely rampant, twining climber which strangles lesser plants quickly. In the right place, such as enveloping a strongly-built but boring shed, it is marvellous, its feathery panicles of creamy, often pink-tinged, flowers appearing from summer well into the autumn and giving this giant a deceptively airy appearance.

Rhodochiton atrosanguineum ○
6m (20ft) · Twining petioles · All summer · Evergreen · Zones 8–10

Usually grown as an annual; sow seed in early spring. Valuable for its dark green, toothed leaves and unusual flowers: red-purple calyces form bells framing the tubular dark purple flower parts. Also successful (although smaller) in a pot. Sunny position.

Schizophragma hydrangeoides ◐○
(JAPANESE HYDRANGEA VINE)
4.5m (15ft) · Self-clinger · Summer · Zones 5–8

Clearly related to *Hydrangea petiolaris; S. hydrangeoides* too produces inflorescences composed of both small, insignificant fertile and larger sterile florets composed of a single petal. The effect is dramatic, each flower-head measuring perhaps a foot across and making a good display after midsummer, for a longer period than the hydrangea's brief fortnight. Like the climbing hydrangea, stems grow away from the wall, so this is not a good choice for a wall with a path running at its foot. The plant flowers most freely in sun.

Solanum crispum 'Glasnevin' ◐○
4.5m (15ft) · Scrambler · Summer · Zones 8–10

On a warm wall, this will quickly make a pretty feature with its clusters of yellow-centred, purple potato flowers held over delicate foliage. The flowering season is long, and the leaves are semi-evergreen.

S. jasminoides 'Album' ◐○
4.5m (15ft) · Twiner · Summer · Zones 9–11

A proper twiner which needs less tying in than the species described above. The white flowers have yellow centres and are freely produced. A warm wall is essential.

Trachelospermum jasminoides ○
(STAR JASMINE)
4.5m (15ft) · Self-clinger · Summer · Evergreen · Zones 8–10

On a sunny wall in a warm climate, this climber is well worth a try. The leaves are dark and shiny and the white flowers, resembling those of jasmine, are sweetly scented. In cooler areas, grow in a conservatory. *T. asiaticum* (zones 7–10) is hardier with creamy white flowers.

Tropaeolum majus (NASTURTIUM) ○
2m (6ft) · Annual · Twiner · Zones 6–9

Familiar plant with its brilliant yellow, orange and red flowers and peppery leaves. There are many varieties available, including one with variegated foliage called 'Alaska', all extremely easy to grow; they can be encouraged to climb and fill an unexpected gap or cheer a new garden. They will self-seed after the first year, and seedlings can be transplanted at whim.

Nasturtiums will also cascade generously down a large retaining wall or bank. Be sure to select the tall varieties for walls, reserving the dwarf types for beds and borders. Sun and well-drained soil.

T. speciosum ◑○
2m (6ft) · Herbaceous perennial · Twiner · Summer · Zones 7–10

Tricky herbaceous climber for cool acid or neutral soils. Its scarlet flowers look startling if it can be encouraged to grow through an evergreen in the shade, but it is not an easy plant.

Vitis (GRAPEVINE) ○
7.5–9m (25–30ft) · Tendrils · Foliage · Zones 5–9

Grapevines are rapid climbers for sunny walls, where their bold foliage is always interesting, often colouring well in autumn.

V. 'Brant' ○
7.5m (25ft) · Foliage and fruit · Zones 6–9

As well as having attractive leaves, 'Brant' also produces bunches of small, sweet, almost scented grapes which are irresistible. In autumn, its leaves turn a subtle dark red patterned with green veins. This is an old Canadian hybrid uniting the American and European types.

V. coignetiae ◑○
9m (30ft) · Foliage · Zones 5–9

This vine has outsize leaves, perhaps up to a foot across, so it makes a bold statement, even in summer; in autumn, when the leaves turn vivid shades of crimson and scarlet, the plant is almost overwhelming. Difficult to accommodate in a small garden, but where there is space this is a marvellous plant. Try growing it with *Clematis orientalis*, whose feathery seed heads make a dramatic contrast.

V. vinifera 'Incana' ○
7.5m (25ft) · Foliage and fruit · Zones 6–9

The Dusty Miller grape has distinctive grey-green leaves with a pale, almost cobweb down. They show up well against old pinkish bricks, but are less successful against pale stone. The fruits are black.

V. vinifera 'Purpurea' ○
7.5m (25ft) · Foliage and fruit · Zones 6–9

These sombre leaves, claret red when young and fading to deep purple, need a pale background or the contrast of silvery leaves, perhaps those of *Cytisus battandieri*, which also needs a sunny wall, to look their best. The purple fruits continue the dark theme.

Wisteria floribunda ◑○
(JAPANESE WISTERIA)
9m (30ft) · Twiner · Early summer · Zones 5–9

Produces the long racemes of scented pea-flowers together with the emerging pale green leaves. The variety 'Alba' has white flowers, whilst 'Macrobotrys' has lilac flowers in enormously long racemes, perhaps three feet long. Wisterias are fast-growing, vigorous plants and they need careful training and pruning to make a well balanced framework and to encourage flowering. They can become rampant in southern regions of North America.

W. sinensis (CHINESE WISTERIA) ◑○
18m (60ft) · Twiner · Late spring-early summer · Zones 5–9

Capable of reaching great heights on the face of a large building, where the supporting wires must be extremely firmly attached. This species produces its generally shorter racemes of fragrant lilac flowers before the leaves appear: a wonderful sight on a venerable specimen with gnarled stems. 'Alba' has white flowers, 'Black Dragon' has double, particularly dark flowers, whilst those of 'Plena' are the same lilac as plain *sinensis*, but doubled into rosettes. The lilac shades have a particular affinity with pale yellow stone.

ROSES

As explained in the main body of the book, climbing roses fall into three categories, the species, the ramblers and the true climbers. They are listed here under these headings. Most roses have at least some thorns, but they have no other special means of climbing; all can be described as scramblers.

Rose hardiness

Specific USDA hardiness zone ratings have not been established for hybrid roses. Instead, they have been given general hardiness ratings which can be roughly equated with the USDA zones as follows:

Hardy: winter hardy without protection to zones 4 or 5
Semi-hardy: winter hardy without protection to zones 6 or 7
Tender: winter hardy without protection to zones 8 or 9

Climbing species

Most of the climbing species are very vigorous and more suited to growing into trees than decorating walls or fences, but there are a few which are not too rampant. Species roses flower only once, but many have decorative fruit and distinctive leaves.

Rosa × *anemonoides* ◑○
3 x 2.5m (10 x 8ft) · Summer · Tender

The large, single, papery pink flowers with their paler edges look extremely delicate and not immediately like roses. Perhaps best on a sunny aspect, but it can do well in sheltered shade.

R. banksiae lutea ○
(YELLOW BANKSIA)
6 x 3m (20 x 10ft) · Late spring · Tender

A rose for a sheltered sunny wall, where it will produce large cascading clusters of small, double, pale yellow flowers in late spring and early summer.

R. banksiae lutescens ○
6 x 3m (20 x 10ft) · Summer · Tender

Also needing a sunny wall, this banksian rose has larger, single flowers with a sweeter, stronger scent. The banksian roses dislike pruning; try not to do it.

R. × *fortuniana* ○
3.5 x 2.5m (12 x 8ft) · Summer · Semi-hardy

Where space is more limited but equally sheltered, try this hybrid which is almost thornless, so easy to prune and train. It has charming, slightly muddled double white flowers with a good scent.

R. laevigata (CHEROKEE ROSE) ○
6 x 4.5m (20 x 15ft) · Hardy

This vigorous rose needs a sunny aspect. Its dark glossy leaves make a good background for the very large, white, single flowers. Grows wild in the southern US.

R. longicuspis ○
9 x 4.5m (30 x 15ft) · Summer · Tender

A less hardy species which needs a large expanse of warm wall. Almost evergreen, with handsome, serrated leaves which are reddish when young. Extremely free-flowering, with huge panicles of medium-sized white (practically scentless), flowers, followed by small orange-red hips.

R. multiflora ◑○
4.5 x 3m (15 x 10ft) · Summer · Hardy

Has a short flowering season, a fault shared by most of the species roses, but when the white flowers appear, they practically obscure the light green leaves. Later there are small oval red hips. This rose is very vigorous and has become naturalized in the eastern US where it can be a bit of a pest. There is a pretty double form, 'Carnea'.

R. soulieana 'Wickwar' ◑○
2.5 x 1.5m (8 x 5ft) · Summer · Tender

A seedling of *R. soulieana* from which derive its pleasing grey-green foliage and upright habit. The flowers are single, pink and very fragrant.

The ramblers

These too flower only once around midsummer, but their single season makes a real highlight in the garden.

'Alberic Barbier' ◑○
4.5 x 3m (15 x 10ft) · Hardy

Good healthy plant with glossy foliage and pliant stems. The semi-double, rather loose flowers are creamy white with a lemon flush.

'Albertine' ○
4.5 x 2.5m (15 x 8ft) · Hardy

A great favourite, because of its sweet scent and pink muddled flowers. The foliage is coppery red when young and the stems are unfortunately armed with copious thorns. Often prone to mildew, but this tends not to strike until after the flowers have faded, and the plant is robust enough to throw it off.

'Alida Lovett' ○
3.5 x 3m (12 x 10ft) · Hardy

Less vigorous than 'Albertine' and easier to deal with as it has far fewer thorns. Large double, pink flowers with a yellow base to each petal.

'American Pillar' ◑○
4.5 x 3m (15 x 10ft) · Hardy

The pink flowers with white eyes are not to everyone's taste; no less a gardener than Vita Sackville-West suggested that this rose and the sugary pink 'Dorothy Perkins' should be 'forever abolished from our gardens'.

'Bobbie James' ◑○
9 x 6m (30 x 20ft) · Hardy

A big plant, usually grown into a tree, but it can look dramatic draped over a high wall, where its trusses of single, cream flowers will cascade in profusion; will tolerate some shade. Good autumn foliage.

'Dorothy Perkins' ○
3 x 2.5m (10 x 8ft) · Hardy

Very familiar rose with masses of small, double, sugary-pink flowers which appear rather later than most ramblers. Rather prone to mildew and the flowers tend to fade and brown rather than shed their petals, so although it is often seen in cottage gardens, there are better roses.

'Emily Gray' ◑○
4.5 x 3m (15 x 10ft) · Hardy

Good yellow rose: the shapely double flowers pale to lemon with age and are very fragrant. A vigorous, healthy plant with shiny foliage.

'Félicité et Perpétue' ◑○
4.5 x 3m (15 x 10ft) · Tender

Later flowering than many ramblers, the creamy, globular, scented blossoms, often with a hint of pink, contrast well with the dark, often evergreen foliage.

'François Juranville' ◑○
4.5 x 3m (15 x 10ft) · Hardy

A good 'Albertine' look-alike, with more tangled petals but similar colouring: pink dipped in weak tea. An excellent display when in full bloom, with the advantage of few thorns.

'Goldfinch' ◑○
2.5 x 1.5m (8 x 5ft) · Hardy

Good plant for a smaller space, with its healthy foliage and semi-double, sweetly scented flowers which combine deep and pale yellow.

'Seagull' ◑○
7.5 x 4.5m (25 x 15ft) · Hardy

Big plant which tolerates a north wall, lightening it with its grey-green leaves and large clusters of highly scented white flowers.

'Wedding Day' ◑○
9 x 4.5m (30 x 15ft) · Hardy

Another rampant rose; bright green, shiny foliage and green, almost thornless wood. Single white flowers with yellow stamens. Tolerates shade and poorer soils.

The climbers

These are almost all repeat-flowering, usually beginning with a generous display which is followed by sparser blooms.

'Alister Stella Gray' ◑○
4.5 x 3m (15 x 10ft) · Tender

Shapely double yellow flowers with deeper centres and paling with age to creamy white. Good scent and long season, with scattered blooms later. Vigorous but easy to train, having pliant branches and few thorns.

'Blairi No. 2' ○
3.5 x 2.5m (12 x 8ft) · Semi-hardy

A rose with an opulent, old-fashioned air and a lovely scent. Pale pink, double, flattish blooms with deeper centres are freely and repeatedly produced.

'Etoile de Hollande' ○
3.5 x 2.5m (12 x 8ft) · Semi-hardy

If you want a red rose, this is excellent with velvet, crimson flowers and a strong sweet scent. It flowers only once; thereafter one can enjoy the plum-coloured new shoots.

'Gloire de Dijon' ○
3.5 x 2.5m (12 x 8ft) · Tender

Beautiful old rose with double flowers which open flat and quartered, tinted with gentle shades of buff and apricot; good tea scent. Flowers mainly in summer but occasional blooms later. Probably best if given a slightly sheltered position: the flowers can be disfigured by rain. Blackspot can be a problem in late summer, but this rose is worth a little extra trouble.

'Golden Showers' ◑○
3 x 2m (10 x 6ft) · Semi-hardy

This has none of the subtlety of 'Gloire de Dijon' but has a robust charm none the less. The large, loose, rather untidy flowers are a good clear yellow and appear pretty well continuously from summer to late autumn above healthy, rich green foliage.

'Lawrence Johnston' ◑○
7.5 x 6m (25 x 20ft) · Hardy

Another semi-double yellow, but much more vigorous and suitable for a large north wall. Summer flowering only.

'Leverkusen' ◑○
3 x 2.5m (10 x 8ft) · Hardy

My favourite yellow rose, with rather pale, very double flowers on an extremely healthy plant. It flowers continuously and will grow in shade if necessary.

'Mermaid' ◑○
9 x 7.5m (30 x 25ft) · Tender

Large and vigorous with notable, dark almost evergreen foliage and distinctive single yellow flowers with their central masses of orange-brown stamens. Will be damaged in a hard winter, so offer a sheltered position, not necessarily in the sun. Has been grown successfully on a wall as far north as Philadelphia.

'Mme Alfred Carrière' ◑○
4.5 x 3m (15 x 10ft) · Semi-hardy

Excellent for a north wall, where its pink-white, double flowers will show up well. It grows vigorously and has few thorns; the wonderfully scented flowers appear throughout summer and into the autumn.

'Mme Grégoire Staechelin' ◑○
4.5 x 3m (15 x 10ft) · Semi-hardy

On a large wall, this vigorous, healthy climber makes a lovely display. Large pale pink flowers, deeper on the outside and with noticeable veins at the edges. Large orange hips are a bonus in autumn if the plant is not dead-headed. Sun or shade.

'New Dawn' ◑○
3 x 2.5m (10 x 8ft) · Hardy

Excellent, producing blush-pink flowers continuously over a long season, beginning a little later than most. Very healthy, with few thorns and a pretty habit of dropping petals before they fade, littering the garden with pale confetti.

'Pompon de Paris' ○
3.5 x 2m (12 x 6ft) · Hardy

An odd creature, but fascinating with its twiggy growth and small pointed leaves. The double, bright pink flowers are almost like buttons.

'Zéphirine Drouhin' ◑○
3 x 2m (10 x 6ft) · Semi-hardy

The famous 'thornless rose'. Bright cerise pink flowers, very double and scented, are produced over a long season, from summer into the autumn.

SHRUBS

It is impossible to give precise sizes for the plants listed below, as so much depends upon growing conditions. Instead, sizes are given as dwarf (**30–60cm/1–2ft**), small (**90–150cm/ 3–5ft**), medium (**1.5–3m/5–10ft**), and large (**over 3m/10ft**). Use these to compare plants, rather than as absolutes. All plants are deciduous unless otherwise stated.

Abelia × *grandiflora* ◑○
Medium · Late summer-autumn · Semi-evergreen · Zones 5–9

Good evergreen, whose shiny small leaves have bronzy tints. The small pink and white tubular flowers are scented and freely produced. Deserves a prominent place near the house. 'Edward Goucher' is a hybrid with pink flowers and slightly smaller habit (zones 6–9).

Abutilon megapotamicum ◑○
Medium · Summer-autumn · Zones 9–10

Plant on a south wall or in a conservatory, against a background which will do justice to the odd pendulous flowers with their large red calyces and yellow petals. The form 'Variegatum' has yellow mottling on its green pointed leaves.

A. × *suntense* ○
Medium-large · Early summer · Zones 8–10

Shallow-cupped mallow flowers decorate the felty grey vine-shaped leaves. 'Jermyns' has dark mauve flowers; 'White Charm' is another variety. Fast growing, not particularly long-lived, for a sunny well-drained position.

A. vitifolium ○
Large · Early summer · Zones 8–10

Similar plant, but a little more vigorous; the mauve flowers are flatter. 'Tennant's White' is a good white; 'Veronica Tennant' has mauve flowers. Sun and good drainage.

Acacia dealbata (SILVER WATTLE) ○
Large · Early spring · Zones 8–10

Only hardy in mild areas in the shelter of a

wall, but it quickly makes a large shrub with pale, ferny leaves and beautifully scented fluffy yellow flowers. Not for alkaline soils.

Aloysia triphylla, see Lippia citriodora

Buddleia alternifolia ○
Large · Early summer · Zones 5–10

Fast-growing, like the rest of the buddleias, this plant quickly makes a dense framework of arching branches which are wreathed with small fragrant lilac flowers. If these are trained against a wall, they will cascade forwards generously.

B. fallowiana ○
Medium · Late summer · Zones 9–10

Needs a warm wall. Extremely pale, woolly stems and leaves, against which the pale lavender flowers make a cool picture.

B. × 'Lochinch' ○
Medium · Late summer · Zones 7–9

B. fallowiana is one of 'Lochinch's parents, and it has inherited grey leaves with white undersides, although it is less tender. Grow freestanding against a wall or, if space is limited, try training the new shoots after the spring pruning into a fan. Sun and good drainage.

Camellia ◐○
Medium/Large · Winter/spring · Evergreen · Zones 7–9

Exotic-looking shrubs for acid or neutral soils. Being evergreen, their dark, glossy leaves make an enduring contribution to the garden, whilst the large, symmetrical flowers can have

a perfection which seems unreal. In order to preserve this perfection, do not plant on an east-facing aspect, where morning sunshine might catch frost-covered blooms and increase winter sunburn on foliage. In northern areas the hardiness range can be stretched by training close against a warm wall, particularly a corner. There are tens of named varieties, with varying flower forms encompassing a wide range of colours from white through pinks to deep red; you need a good catalogue to choose properly.

Varieties of C. japonica are most numerous: 'Adolphe Audusson' has large, deep red, semi-double flowers and is among the hardiest; 'Alba Simplex' has large white flowers with conspicuous stamens; 'Pink Perfection' has small, formal, double flowers.

The C. williamsii varieties have smaller leaves and the flowers are mostly pink: 'Donation' has orchid-pink, large, semi-double flowers; 'Francis Hanger' is a single white variety.

The autumn-blooming C. sasanqua has smaller leaves and makes a neat wall shrub, particularly in cool climates where it needs the extra summer heat to bloom well and harden its wood. The flowers open over a long period from October to early winter. Colours range from white through pink to red. Two of the hardiest standard varieties are 'Cleopatra' (pink) and 'Yuletide' (red).

Carpenteria californica ○
Medium · Summer · Evergreen · Zones 8–10

Well-shaped plant for a sunny wall where its light green foliage is covered with white, flattened flowers with yellow anthers for two or three weeks in early summer. Does not need pruning.

Ceanothus (CALIFORNIAN LILAC) ○
Medium/Large · Summer and/or autumn · Some evergreen · Zones 8–10

This family is a valuable one. Most varieties are fast-growing, producing dense panicles of small blue flowers from an early age. The deciduous types are generally hardier than the evergreen. All like a sunny wall and well-drained soil and generally do well in the eastern US.

C. arboreus 'Trewithen Blue'
Late spring · Evergreen

Large leaves and large panicles of deep blue flowers.

C. 'A.T. Johnson'
Spring and autumn · Evergreen

Another good blue with a useful double season.

C. 'Autumnal Blue'
Late summer and autumn · Evergreen

Good hardy variety with deep blue flowers.

C. 'Cascade'
Spring · Evergreen

Looser clusters of bright blue flowers.

C. 'Gloire de Versailles'
Summer and autumn · Deciduous

Large panicles of soft powder-blue flowers.

C. impressus
Spring · Evergreen

A particular favourite because of its small,

deeply veined leaves and dense mass of good blue flowers. 'Puget Blue' is a selected form.

C. thyrsiflorus repens
(see Plants for Retaining Walls, p. 133)

Ceratostigma willmottianum ○
(HARDY PLUMBAGO)
Dwarf · Early autumn · Zones 8–10

Choice plant for a well-drained site, where its rich blue flowers are an unexpected delight at the end of the summer. Earlier in the year, the smooth, light green leaves are held on wiry black stems; the leaves turn bright red before falling. Sometimes cut to the ground by frost, but usually springs up again. Be sure to buy this, rather than the superficially similar but less good *C. griffithii*.

Chaenomeles speciosa and × superba
Medium · Spring · Zones 6–9 ●◑○

The flowering quinces are extremely valuable, hardy, spring-flowering shrubs with a very long season of bloom. Happy in most positions, including shade. The flowers are followed, later in the year, by attractive fruit. Perfectly hardy enough to grow in the open, but the shelter of a wall will encourage early flowering. Allow them to make an informal bush, or train carefully back to a support if space is limited. Any aspect. 'Toyo Nishiki' is a very pretty pink and white variety, reminiscent of apple blossom; 'Nivalis' is a large pure white; 'Hollandia' is semi-double and deep red.

Chimonanthus praecox ◑○
(WINTERSWEET)
Medium · Winter · Zones 7–9

Slow-growing plant which needs a warm wall to ripen its shoots. When mature, it produces waxy yellow flowers with purple centres and a heavy spicy scent. Spoilt by very cold weather; probably too slow and unattractive in summer for a small garden. Good on chalk.

Choisya ternata ◑○
(MEXICAN ORANGE BLOSSOM)
Medium · Early summer · Evergreen · Zones 7–9

Glossy leaves make a fine background for the white, sweetly scented flowers. Makes a pleasing rounded bush which needs the shelter of a warm wall in a cold garden, but can grow happily in the shade of a north wall if the position is not too exposed.

Colutea arborescens ○
(BLADDER SENNA)
Large · Summer · Zones 5–7

A sparse-growing but vigorous legume which has delicate pinnate leaves and yellow pea-flowers over a long season. The inflated seed pods burst in hot sunshine.

Convolvulus cneorum ○
Dwarf · Early summer · Evergreen · Zones 9–10

Will flourish in the dry shelter at the foot of a sunny wall. Its leaves are intensely silky and silvery, and the typical convolvulus flowers open white from pink buds. Good drainage is essential.

Coronilla glauca ○
Small · Winter-spring · Evergreen · Zones 9–10

The bright yellow pea-flowers can appear sporadically throughout the year, but are most profuse in good winter weather and into spring; delicate glaucous leaves. Needs a warm wall and good drainage; the same site suits rosemary, and they look well together.

Cotoneaster ◑○
Small to large · Summer flowers, autumn berries · Some evergreen · Zones 4–8

Most of these hardy berry-bearing shrubs are best grown as free-standing specimens, but a few varieties make good wall plants.

C. bullatus
Large · Zones 5–8

With its large corrugated leaves, this is sometimes placed by a wall to make a solid buttress. The bright red fruits appear early in autumn and the leaves turn various subtle shades of purple and red.

C. dammeri
Small · Evergreen · Zones 5–8

Makes a ground cover unless trained up a wall where it forms a cascade of foliage with red berries in autumn.

C. franchetii
Medium · Semi-evergreen · Zones 5–8

Sage-coloured foliage and attractive orange fruits, and a graceful habit which makes training easy.

C. horizontalis
Dwarf, spreading · Zones 4–8

The habit is almost unbearably stiff, enabling it to climb a wall unaided, but it should be tied in to keep it stable. Bears rich red berries in late summer, and a frosty autumn will turn the leaves a similar colour for several weeks. Best in sun.

C. salicifolius
Variable height · Evergreen · Zones 6–8

Variable species ranging in habit from upright to trailing; all can be trained on a wall. 'Autumn Fire', 'Repens' and 'Scarlet Leader' are all groundcover types suitable for training up a wall similarly to *C. dammeri*.

Cytisus battandieri ○
Large · Summer · Zones 8–9

This silvery-leaved member of the broom family bears pineapple-scented yellow flowers in short spikes rather like a tubby lupin. Needs good drainage and a warm wall. Makes a good contrast for dark leaves; see *Vitis* in the climbers section.

Forsythia suspensa 'Nymans' ◑○
Large · Spring · Zones 5–9

Delicate shrub with arching branches bearing well-spaced primrose coloured flowers – not at all like the congested, stiff forsythias one usually envisages. Can be trained up a high wall or can cascade down a high retaining wall. Part shade.

Fremontodendron californicum ○
Large · Summer · Evergreen · Zones 9–10

Fast-growing plant with leathery, three-lobed leaves, felted beneath. The large yellow flowers are actually petal-less, the colour being provided over a long season by conspicuous sepals. Must have a warm wall and good drainage; will grow on chalk.

Garrya elliptica (SILK TASSEL BUSH) ◑
Large · Winter · Evergreen · Zones 8–9

Choose a male plant, preferably the named form 'James Roof', which will bear long grey-green catkins after Christmas. Will grow happily on a north wall, but its leathery leaves need protection from icy winds. A large and rather boring plant for the rest of the year, one can only really accommodate it in a spacious garden.

Hydrangea quercifolia ○
(OAK-LEAF HYDRANGEA)
Medium · Late summer · Zones 5–9

Bold plant with large, deeply cut leaves. The variety 'Snow Queen' is a superior form, with large conical heads of white sterile florets which gradually fade to pink. The dramatic foliage turns deep red-purple in autumn. Only seen at its best in a warm sheltered spot, or in a climate with reliably hot summers.

Hydrangea villosa ◑○
Medium · Late summer · Zones 7–9

Not usually a wall shrub, but where there is space it makes a useful mass in a dark corner. The large leaves are softly hairy and the lilac lace-cap flowers appear over several weeks,

remaining attractive even when they have faded. Thrives in most conditions, and, in cool climates, is happy in sun as well as shade. A variable species, but some forms are hardy in zone 6.

Jasminum nudiflorum ◑○
(WINTER JASMINE)
Medium/large · Winter · Zones 6–10

One of the great stalwarts of the winter garden, producing masses of starry yellow flowers throughout the season. Hard frost will damage the flowers, but there is a succession of buds to replace the spoilt display and these open immediately if one picks sprays for the house. A sprawling shrub, but usually seen against a wall – it is perfectly happy facing north. In some ways a tricky plant to train – one often sees it collapsed into an informal mound, but it can be controlled by tying in the long angular shoots as they appear. Cut back flowered shoots in spring.

Kerria japonica ◑
Medium · Late spring · Zones 4–9

A suckering shrub with attractive green stems and rich yellow flowers. The double form is most often seen, but the single flowers are prettier, I think. 'Picta' is an attractive variety with white-edged leaves, useful to brighten a dull area. Flowers best in sun but can survive in shade. A tough and easy plant.

Lagerstroemia indica (CRAPE MYRTLE) ○
Large · Late summer · Zones 7–9

Lilac-pink flowers and an attractively mottled pink and grey trunk. In the southern US this standard landscape plant may become tree-like. New hybrids are hardier and include: 'Acoma', pink, semi-dwarf; 'Natchez', white with exceptional bark; 'Powhatan', purple.

Laurus nobilis (BAY LAUREL) ◑○
Large · Foliage · Evergreen · Zones 8–10

A lovely plant with aromatic foliage (the culinary bay), which needs a warm wall for protection. Clip it into a formal shape or let it grow into a tall mass.

Lavatera olbia 'Rosea' ○
(TREE MALLOW)
Medium · Summer-autumn · Zones 7–9

Usefully fast grower with grey-green leaves and a long succession of pink hollyhock flowers. It does not necessarily need the shelter of a wall, but it can give a quick boost to a new border, and will flourish in the sunshine and warmth of a south or west wall. The variety 'Barnsley' is a relatively recent introduction: it has more striking flowers, white with red centres, gradually fading to pink.

Lippia citriodora, syn. Aloysia triphylla
(LEMON VERBENA) ○
Medium · Summer · Scented foliage · Zones 8–10

Insignificant white to very pale purple flowers, but the point of growing it is to enjoy the sharp lemon scent of its long tapering leaves; plant it where you can pinch them to release the fragrance. Needs a warm position and well-drained soil.

Magnolia grandiflora ◑○
Large · Early summer · Evergreen · Zones 7–10

With the stature of a tree, requires a large sunny wall. The big glossy leaves are magnificent, and the huge cream flowers have thick sensuous petals and a heavy lemony scent. Choose one of the named varieties which will flower at an earlier age than seedlings: 'Little Gem' makes a charming wall subject with its smaller leaves and flowers and neat habit. 'St Mary' does not grow as vigorously as most varieties, though it has the potential to make a sizeable tree and has very attractive foliage with heavy brown undersides. 'Edith Bogue' is the hardiest known variety (zone 6), but has stiff, less compact growth; use on a wall only when extra hardiness is needed.

M. sieboldii ◑○
Large · All summer · Zones 6–8

Not such a giant as M. grandiflora but nevertheless a wide-spreading shrub which needs space in front of the wall as well as on it. Its pendant white, scented flowers have crimson stamens and appear intermittently throughout summer. Good red clusters of fruit in autumn.

M. wilsonii ◑
Large · Early summer · Zones 7–8

Another wide spreader with down-turned white flowers. Needs partial shade.

Myrtus communis (MYRTLE) ◑○
Large · Late summer · Evergreen · Zones 8–10

Small, pointed aromatic leaves and fluffy white flowers in late summer and autumn. It makes a dense mass of close-packed leaves and flowers in great profusion; bluish-black berries. Especially good in mild coastal areas, where the waxy leaves resist salt spray, but needing the protection of a warm wall elsewhere. The form 'Tarentina' has narrower leaves and white berries; it is reckoned to be hardier.

Phygelius capensis (CAPE FIGWORT) ○
Medium · Late summer · Zones 8–9

South African plant usually classed as a sub-shrub, dying back to ground level over winter, but against a warm wall the aerial parts can survive, giving it a head start the next season. An airy plant, which throws up long brown stems set sparsely with drooping, tubular, coral-coloured flowers.

Piptanthus laburnifolius ○
(EVERGREEN LABURNUM)
Large · Early summer · Evergreen · Zones 8–9

Fast-growing shrub for a sunny position. Green stems and dark trifoliate leaves, against which the bright yellow pea-flowers make a strong contrast. Seed pods appear later; they are not particularly decorative.

Pittosporum tenuifolium ◑
Large · Foliage · Evergreen · Zones 8–10

Attractive plant whose glossy, pale green, crinkly leaves set on black shoots are popular with flower arrangers. Hardy in coastal areas, but inland will need the shelter of a wall. 'Garnettii' has grey-green leaves with white margins and a pink flush in winter. Makes a neat shape without clipping.

Pyracantha (FIRETHORN) ◑○
Medium to large · Summer · Evergreen · Zones 5–9

The firethorns are well-named. These prickly shrubs produce small white flowers in summer and masses of hot-coloured berries in shades of red, orange and yellow in the autumn. Many keep their berries for a considerable time. *P. angustifolia* (zones 7–9) has narrow leaves with grey felt beneath, and orange-yellow persistent fruits. *P. coccinea* 'Lalandei' (zone 5) is more vigorous with an erect habit and prolific large orange-red fruits. *P. rogersiana* 'Flava' (zones 7–9) is large with narrow leaves and bright yellow fruits. See a good catalogue for the full range. Sun or shade.

Teucrium fruticans (TREE GERMANDER)
Small · Summer · Evergreen · Zones 8–9 ○

Rather tender, needing well-drained soil and the warmth of a wall to flourish, this is an airy, silvery-leaved plant with pale blue flowers throughout the summer. The form 'Azureum' has deeper blue flowers but is even less hardy. Lovely with pale pink roses and other silver leaves.

Viburnum carlesii ◑○
(KOREAN SPICEBUSH)
Large · Spring · Zones 4–8

Clustered pink buds open to white flowers which scent the air with one of the finest fragrances of the spring garden. *V. x juddii* is easier to grow and just as fragrant. *V. x burkwoodii* is not quite so scented.

V. opulus ◑○
(GUELDER ROSE)
Large · Summer · Zones 3–8

A lovely tough plant to cheer a dark wall. White flowers like a lacecap hydrangea, followed by jewel-like translucent red fruit in autumn. Choose the variety 'Compactum' if

space is limited, or 'Xanthocarpum' if you prefer yellow berries. A native of damp places, but thrives in ordinary well-drained soil as well. *V. trilobum* is a similar American native which is hardier (zones 2–8) and more resistant to aphids.

V. plicatum tomentosum ◑○
(DOUBLEFILE VIBURNUM)
Medium · Spring · Zones 4–8

The layered habit of growth is superbly suited for espaliering on a wall. 'Shasta' is slightly less vigorous and has larger flowers.

V. rhytidophyllum ◑
(LEATHERLEAF VIBURNUM)
Large · Spring · Semi-evergreen · Zones 5–8

The large narrow leaves and flat flower clusters are a spectacle when trained against a wall. The hybrid *V. x pragense* is fully evergreen but has smaller leaves.

FRUIT

Rootstocks for fruit
The most common reason for grafting fruit varieties on special rootstocks is to dwarf the size of the tree. Other factors to consider in selection of a specific rootstock include drought tolerance and physical strength to support the tree, which is less of a factor for espaliers. New and improved types are being developed in Europe and America but, at the present, the following mentioned for each fruit are generally recommended. Consult your local Extension Service for the latest recommendations.

Apples ○
APPLE ROOTSTOCKS

M9: Very dwarf, for 2.5–2.75m (8–9ft) tree; unstable roots. Fire blight susceptible in warm climates.
M26: dwarf, about 3.5m (12ft); perhaps the best for general garden use.
MM106: semi-dwarf, for trees 4.5–5.5m (15–18ft); roots give stronger support to tree.

Apples may be grown as espaliers, fans, or cordons, depending on the space available, and usually on a semi-dwarfing rootstock such as MM106. Even on the same rootstock, different varieties show varying degrees of vigour, but a spacing of 3.5m–4.5m (12–15ft) between espaliers or fans would be about right. Cordons can obviously be grown closer together, say 60–90cm (2–3ft) between plants on MM106; as little as 45–60cm (18–24in) between plants on the dwarfing M9. There is a wide variety of apples available from specialist nurseries and some of the older kinds are more suited to growing in a garden than on a commercial scale.

Apples do not usually need the warmth of a south wall, as they are perfectly hardy; a west wall is probably best, although some of the later-flowering varieties could do well facing east. Most need a pollinator (some varieties need two) to set fruit.

The following is a brief selection. For more details, consult the catalogue of a specialist fruit grower, see list of suppliers, p.155.
EMPIRE: dessert. Improved McIntosh with a redder skin; resistant to fire blight and cedar-apple rust. Ripens mid-September. Grows better in south; zones 4–7.
LIBERTY: dessert. New McIntosh type. Immune to scab and cedar rust; resistant to fire

blight and mildew. Prolific. Ripens early September and stores well. Zones 4–6.

PRIMA: dessert, cooker. New variety resistant to fire blight, mildew and scab. Ripens late August, stores well. Zones 5–8.

PRISCILLA: dessert. New variety resistant to scab, fire blight and cedar rust. Pollinates Prima. Ripens mid-September. Zones 5–8.

Pears ○

PEAR ROOTSTOCKS

Quince rootstocks are used for dwarfing pears but are generally less hardy in the north where pear seedlings must be used. The most commonly recommended dwarfing stocks are Provence which is the preferred type in N. America, and Quince A which is used on both sides of the Atlantic.

Pears are less hardy than apples, and flower rather earlier, so they do best in the shelter of a west or even a south wall. On dwarfing rootstocks, pears are sufficiently reduced in vigour to be accommodated in a smaller garden. Grow as espaliers, fans or cordons. Plant espaliers or fans 3.5–4.5m (12–15ft) apart; cordons 60–90cm (2–3ft) from each other. Like apples, pears need a pollinator.

DOYENNE DU COMICE: said to be the best pear of all, but not absolutely reliable. Give it a warm wall and spray regularly against scab; the fruit is ready to eat in late autumn. Pollinated by any of the above varieties. Zones 5–7.

KIEFFER: large yellow fruit mid-October which is resistant to fire blight and stores well. Exceptionally adaptable to the north and south. Zones 4–9.

Plums ○

Most plums do best on a warm west wall. In North America the European plums do best in the north-east, while the Japanese types are best for the south and west. There are two main rootstocks: the widely used St Julien A, which is suitable for fans, and the newer, more dwarfing Pixy, on which cordons are possible. Plant fans 3.5m (12 ft) apart, cordons 60–90cm (2–3ft) from each other. Some varieties are self-fertile, others need a pollinator.

The European types have oval, usually purple, fruit with firmer, less juicy flesh. Prune plums have a high sugar and low water content suitable for drying.

EARLIBLUE: well-flavoured with soft flesh, freestone. Similar to Stanley; later bloom reduces frost danger. Self-fertile. Late July. Zones 5–8.

STANLEY: the best-known variety. Prune type, excellent for eating fresh, canning or drying. Purple skin, golden flesh, freestone. Recommended for the north-east, mid-west and upper south. Not compatible with St Julien A rootstock. Early September. Zones 5–8.

The Japanese types have round, juicy, black, red or yellow fruit; clingstone. They stand southern summer heat better, but some have very low winter chilling requirements. Not self-pollinating. Zones 6–9, warmer parts of zone 5.

RED HEART: large, juicy red fruit with red flesh. Can be used fresh, canned or in preserves. Early August. Pollinator: Shiro. Zones 5–9.

SHIRO: good-flavoured golden plum for eating fresh or canning. Ready late July. Pollinate with Red Heart. Zones 5–9.

Apricots, nectarines and peaches ○

Apricots grow easily in the open in the US. They should be trained as fans, and planted about 6m (20ft) apart. All are self-fertile, but the early flowering season means that the blossom might need protection, in the form of fine netting, from frost. Pollinating insects will also be scarce in a cold spell, so it is worth pollinating by hand, using a small paint brush or ball of cotton wool on a stick.

Apricots are vigorous trees but they are available on St Julien A which restricts their size. 'Moorpark' (zones 5-8) is the most widely available cultivar, and it crops in August and September. 'Goldcot' is one of the hardiest varieties (zones 5-8).

Nectarines (zones 5-8) are like smooth-skinned peaches, if perhaps a little less robust. 'Mericrest' is an early variety ripening in early August; it is richly-flavoured and one of the hardiest varieties. 'Redgold' is ready a little later in mid-August, and resists late spring frosts.

Peaches (zones 5-8) 'Red Haven' produces fruit by early July, yellow, ripening to red. 'Elberta' is a slightly later variety, and has been a favourite for years. 'Madison' is especially hardy with yellow flesh and a red blush.

Dwarfing rootstocks are not successful for nectarines and peaches in most of the US – only for the warmest areas, such as California.

Cherries ◑○

CHERRY ROOTSTOCK

'Colt' the most commonly recommended dwarfing rootstock in both Britain and N. America. Dwarfs to about three–quarters of the tree's normal size. Not hardy north of zone 6.

Sweet cherries are so attractive to birds that

there is no point in growing them unless they can be netted for protection. A recent introduction is the variety 'Compact Stella' (zones 5–9), which is self-fertile and much smaller than previously available kinds. Give it a warm wall, train as a fan, and do remember to net before the fruit ripens.

The 'Morello' cherry (zones 5–8) has long been a standby for north walls, where it looks lovely in flower and where the acid fruit ripens perfectly well. Self-fertile. Fruit is borne on young shoots, made the previous summer.

Figs ○

Figs would probably be grown even if they never fruited, simply for the sake of their huge leathery leaves, but to give a fig the best chance of ripening fruit in cool climates, plant it in a warm corner with its roots restricted by a layer of rubble or some other device. Train as a fan to allow sunlight to reach all the branches. In northern climates (zone 6) figs must be wrapped with a good insulating material and covered to keep the branches dry. If fruit is desired the following summer, some of the branches must survive the winter.

'Brown Turkey' (zones 7–10) is the most reliable variety for winter hardiness or a cool climate. It ripens to a deep chocolate colour with red flesh. 'Brunswick' (zones 5–9) has larger, greener fruit.

Grapevines ○

Grapes can be grown as cordons or espaliers, on a warm south wall. A grapevine can be kept to the size you want it, but most will make large features if allowed to, so I would allow 4.5m (15ft) between neighbouring plants. The decorative and edible variety 'Brant' has been described earlier (p.121). In north-eastern America, the American or fox grapes (zones 5–8) grow best. 'Concord' is the most popular with deep blue fruit, but white and pink varieties are also available. European grapes (zones 7–9) are better suited to the south-western states, especially California. 'Emperor' with red flesh and 'Thompson Seedless' with seedless green fruit are some of the most popular.

Kiwi fruit (zones 7–9)

This vigorous climber is suitable for a south or west wall. Though twining, it should be pruned in a fashion similar to grapes and must be tied into wires. Happy in ordinary garden soil. Female plants bear the fruit, but they need a male nearby to act as pollinator: one male will be sufficient for up to half a dozen females (should you have the space). Plant roughly 2–2.5m (6–8ft) apart.

Soft fruit
RED AND WHITE CURRANTS AND GOOSEBERRIES

These will both thrive on a north wall so are particularly useful for a small space where a Morello cherry would be too vigorous. The currants are best trained as single upright cordons planted 30–45cm (12–18in) apart; they produce most of their fruit on short spurs on older wood. Gooseberries can be fan-trained or grown as cordons: fans should stand 120cm (4ft) apart, cordons 45–60cm (18–24in). Fruit bushes can also be used as hedges; see the section on Informal Hedges, p.106.

Cultivation of currants and gooseberries is prohibited in parts of America because they are the alternate host of White Pine blister rust.

BLACKBERRIES (zones 5–8)

I still think that the best flavour is found in wild blackberries collected from the hedgerow, but for garden cultivation it is hard to beat the easy-to-handle 'Oregon Thornless Blackberry'. This is a decorative plant to train up a reasonably sunny wall; it has finely cut leaves so it looks handsome even when not in flower or fruit. Cut back newly-planted canes to 15cm (6in) and tie in the pliant new canes as they grow. Cut out old canes after harvesting the fruit.

PLANTS FOR RETAINING WALLS

The plants described here cover a range of categories: alpines, hardy perennials, small shrubs and ferns. The choice is a personal one, because so many plants can be used on, in or below a retaining wall that it would be impossible to cover them all. Again, it is difficult to give exact dimensions, because so much depends on the growing conditions; rather, I have indicated relative size: small (less than **15cm/6in**); medium (**15–60cm/6–24in**); and large (**60–120cm/2–4ft**), with a mention if a plant is particularly tall or aggressive as a spreader or self-seeder. In a small wall, these are the last plants one wants, but they can come into their own in a larger space where one does not want to garden in detail and where, in any case, bolder planting is more effective.

Acaena 'BLUE HAZE' ○
Small, vigorous carpeter · Late summer · Evergreen · Zones 7-9

Serrated bluish foliage and small brownish burr-like flowers. Needs full sun and good drainage, but resents excessive heat.

Adiantum pedatum ●
Fern · Small · Zones 3–8

A hardy type of maidenhair fern, with delicate fronds held above long slender stems. Give it a shady, damp position. *A. venustum* is delicate too, but it creates a more effective carpet, if this is your aim.

Ajuga reptans ●
Groundcover · Small, carpeting · Late spring · Evergreen · Zones 2–10

There are several cultivars of this pretty, slowly-spreading plant; all prefer some moisture in the soil and will grow in part shade. 'Purpurea' is rather sombre, with its dark wine-red leaves, although the small blue flower spikes lighten it somewhat. 'Variegata' has leaves marked with creamy buff.

Alchemilla mollis ◑○
(LADY'S MANTLE)
Herbaceous perennial · Medium · Summer · Zones 3–8

Very easy plant for sun or shade, seeding itself almost too readily if not dead-headed after the foamy, acid-green flowers have faded. But undoubtedly charming with its rounded, velvety leaves which hold drops of water so prettily in their centres. Use alchemilla *en masse* to bring coherence to a large expanse of wall, in sun or shade, and enjoy its robustness and fecundity.

Alyssum saxatile ◑○
Rock plant · Medium · Spring · Evergreen · Zones 4–9

This familiar spring plant, so often teamed with aubrieta, occurs in various forms, of which 'Citrinum' has the softest yellow flowers well matched by grey mounds of foliage. Cut

back after flowering. Full sun and good drainage.

Anemone × *hybrida* ◑○
(JAPANESE ANEMONE)
Herbaceous perennial · Tall · Late summer · Zones 6–9

This may seem an odd choice, but the mildly running rootstock can colonize the foot of a partly shaded wall and throw up a prolonged succession of flowers on tall, self-supporting stems. The flowers are purplish pink, but there are several named varieties, such as the clear white 'Honorine Jobert', whose flowers are decorated with a mass of yellow stamens. *A. hupehensis* is hardier and earlier flowering.

Anthemis cupaniana ○
Rock plant · Medium, spreading · Early summer · Evergreen · Zones 5–9

Spreading daisy with finely-cut silver leaves, which becomes woody with age. It is then worth taking cuttings and starting again; the young plants are better clothed with foliage and altogether more presentable. A lovely thing for a sunny wall-face.

Arabis caucasica 'Flore Pleno' ◑○
Rock plant · Small · Spring · Evergreen · Zones 4–8

Cottagey alpine, with double white flowers over low foliage which spreads quite quickly but is not invasive. Flowers for much longer than the common single form. Sun.

Asplenium scolopendrium ●
(HART'S TONGUE FERN)
Fern · Medium · Evergreen · Zones 3–8

Splendid broad green leaves which are espe-

cially fresh in the spring. Needs some shade and a degree of moisture, but will tolerate chalk so is useful on a limy soil. Attractive in the face of a wall or at its foot. Also known as *A. phyllitis*.

A. trichomanes ●◑○
(MAIDENHAIR SPLEENWORT)
Fern · Small · Zones 3–8

Will grow even in a sunny wall face, where it will make a hardy clump. Its wiry black stems bear lobed green leaves.

Athyrium filix-femina (LADY FERN) ●◑
Fern · Large · Zones 3–8

A native in both Britain and America commonly found in woodland. Its tall lacy fronds are most decorative; give the plant shade and moisture and preferably some leaf-mould, to mimic its preferred habitat. There are many interesting dwarf and foliage forms also available.

Aubrieta ◑○
Rock plant · Small · Spring · Evergreen · Zones 4–8

The washed-out mauve shades of aubrieta are surely familiar even to non-gardeners, as they spread generously over rock gardens in spring together with their almost constant companions, the alyssums. There are named varieties, though, which have more distinct colours: 'Bressingham Pink' has double, clear pink flowers, 'Henslow Purple' is a strong shade and 'Variegata' has green and cream leaves which show off the almost blue flowers. Aubrietas should be clipped back after flowering but otherwise allowed to trail. Choose a spot sheltered from afternoon heat in hot climates.

Blechnum penna marina ◑
Fern · Small · Evergreen · Zones 6–9

A useful dwarf fern for wall crevices in cool climates, in sun or shade.

Campanula (BELLFLOWER) ◑○
Rock plant · Small · Summer · Evergreen

Alpine varieties of the large campanula family are very useful on sunny or partly shaded walls.

C. carpatica
(Zones 3–8)

This particular species makes tufted cushions which are covered with upturned bell flowers in summer. 'Blue Moonlight' is light blue, 'Chewton Joy' is darker and later, while 'Hannah' carries white flowers over a long season. *C.c. turbinata* is perhaps the best dwarf campanula because of its tidy clump-forming habit and long season of saucer-shaped, rich blue flowers. 'Alba' is not quite white, but very pale blue with a darker centre.

C. cochlearifolia
Zones 6–9

A pretty thing with small dangling bell flowers on 10cm (4in) stems. There are white as well as blue and double blue forms.

C. garganica
Zones 6–8

This has a more spreading habit, sending out trailing stems set with blue flowers. 'W.H. Paine' is a selected, deep blue form.

Ceanothus thyrsiflorus repens ◑○
Shrub · Large · Early summer · Evergreen · Zones 8–9

Prostrate shrub which quickly forms an evergreen mound. The light blue flowers are freely produced (although occasionally a specimen is shy to flower), making a satisfying, well-clothed cushion. Use a pair of them to frame steps or a doorway, and plant later-flowering clematis such as the small-flowered *C. viticella* 'Alba Luxurians' to trail through and over the shrubs' branches.

Centranthus ruber (VALERIAN) ◑○
Herbaceous perennial · Medium · Summer · Zones 4–9

A lovely wall plant, as long as the wall is sound; valerian has long roots which become thick with age and they can easily weaken the entire structure. The ordinary form has rather dirty red flowers, so look for the good white or true warm pink, or the named red 'Atrococcineus'. The leaves are rather fleshy and the tiny flowers are held in dense inflorescences on 45cm (18in) stems. The wind-blown seed settles and germinates in suitable crannies.

Cerastium tomentosum columnae ◑○
(SNOW-IN-SUMMER)
Rock plant · Small · Summer · Evergreen · Zones 3–7

Safe, non-spreading form of *C. tomentosum*: a pretty thing for full sun with very silvery leaves and masses of open white flowers. Do not allow *C. tomentosum* itself into the garden, unless you wish to grow nothing else – its white roots are extremely invasive.

Cistus (SUN ROSE) ○
Shrub · Medium · Summer · Evergreen · Zones 8–10

Most of the sun roses are too large to use on top of a retaining wall, but there are one or two smaller varieties which will revel in the sun and good drainage it provides. They are evergreens, often with aromatic leaves, and with frail-looking, papery flowers. *C. × lusitanicus* 'Decumbens' is a wide-spreading variety with large white flowers marked with crimson basal blotches. *C.* 'Silver Pink' is a reliably hardy kind, with grey leaves and masses of pale pink flowers. They grow best on the Pacific coast.

Corydalis lutea ◑○
Rock plant · Small · Summer · Zones 5–8

Finely cut glaucous, almost succulent foliage is the foil for small yellow flowers. A plant which could prove hard to eradicate, because it is able to root in the tiniest cracks, it is nevertheless charming – not at all like a weed in appearance.

Cotyledon simplicifolia ◑
Rock plant · Small · Summer · Evergreen · Zones 5–7

Good plant for half shade and generally poor conditions; rounded, succulent, bronzy-green leaves and slender stems decorated very freely with small yellow flowers.

Cytisus × kewensis ○
Shrub · Medium · Early summer · Zones 6–9

Semi-prostrate broom with typically green stems and flattened, insignificant leaves. Creamy yellow flowers are produced in abundance, albeit for a relatively short-lived display and the plant looks good draping the top of a wall. Add later interest by planting *Geranium wallichianum* 'Buxton's Variety' (see below), close by.

Dianthus (PINKS) ○
Rock plant/herbaceous perennial · Small to medium · Summer · Evergreen · Zones 3–9 depending on variety, many hardy to Zone 4, few to 3.

There are dwarf varieties as well as the long-stemmed carnations, and they all like the sharp drainage of the top and face of a sunny wall. They gradually hang down to make (usually) glaucous masses of narrow foliage set with scented flowers. The smaller species such as *D. neglectus* (zones 5–9) are obviously ideal for a low wall full of treasures; the larger ones better for making a larger-scale impact. 'Mrs Sinkins' is a good double white, very scented; 'Charles Musgrave' is a single white with a green eye; 'Inchmery' is a plain pink. The 'Old Crimson Clove' carnation is deep red and has a strong sweet scent. There are a great many other named varieties; consult a specialist catalogue.

Digitalis purpurea (FOXGLOVE) ●◐○
Biennial · Tall · Early summer · Zones 4–9

A woodland plant which enjoys the shade and moisture at the bottom of the shady retaining wall. Rosettes of softly hairy leaves send up tall spikes of flower in the second year, which should be allowed to set seed. Thereafter, the entire plant can be pulled out to reveal the wall again. The usual form has purple flowers, but there is a white variety, and seed companies can also supply the lovely apricot foxglove, which is equally easy and

which looks marvellous against yellowish stone.

Dryopteris filix-mas crispa cristata ●
Fern · Medium · Zones 3–10

This frilly-edged form of the male fern has dense green spreading fronds. Give it shade and moisture.

Erigeron karvinskianus ○
Herbaceous perennial · Small · All summer · Zones 9–10

A marvellous Mexican daisy which can be hard to obtain and establish, but which will seed generously and spread everywhere if one manages to install a plant. The foliage is divided and generally unobtrusive; the small white daisy flowers, tinged with pink, are held on slender, wiry stems. There will be flowers until the frosts.

Erinus alpinus (FAIRY FOXGLOVE) ◐○
Rock plant · Small · Summer · Evergreen · Zones 4–9

A small plant, but it can seed itself widely to make a large-scale display. It forms a small mat of green foliage, only a few inches across, above which rise little spikes of rose-purple flowers. There is a white variety. Recommended for shade in hot summers in the US.

Erysimum linifolium ◐○
Rock plant · Medium · Summer · Evergreen · Zones 6–8

The shrubby wallflowers like the well-drained top or face of a sunny wall and they bear flowers over a long period from early summer. 'Bowles' Mauve' is a good larger variety. 'Moonlight' has pale yellow flowers, and 'Mutabilis' has flowers which change colour as

they age, encompassing shades of yellow, brown, warm wine red and purple. All must be propagated by cuttings, so are tricky to establish in an existing wall face; try growing them in peat pots which can then be wedged into spaces between stones. Cuttings should be taken as a matter of routine, to replace winter losses and older, leggy specimens. Often listed under *Cheiranthus*.

Euphorbia myrsinites ◐○
Rock plant · Medium · Late spring · Evergreen · Zones 5–9

Very glaucous trailing plant, with succulent leaves to decorate the top of a sunny wall. The sulphur-yellow bracts are the showiest part of the flower.

E. robbiae ●◐○
Herbaceous perennial · Medium · Late spring · Evergreen · Zones 7–9

A very different plant from *E. myrsinites*, this spurge has dark leaves and an upright habit. It bears lime-green flowers in spring, and the showy bracts persist. Good in sun, but especially useful in poor soil in shade. The roots run mildly.

Genista lydia ○
Shrub · Large · Early summer · Zones 7–9

This spreading shrub carries a dense crop of bright yellow pea-flowers which practically obscure the dark green mound of its stems and foliage. Another plant for the top of a significant wall in full sun; it may only reach 90cm (3ft) in height but can spread considerably more. Add a late-flowering clematis to improve its off season.

Geranium cinereum 'Ballerina' ◑○

Rock plant · Small · Early summer · Evergreen · Zones 5–8

A dwarf cranesbill with pretty foliage and lilac pink flowers with contrasting red veins and centres.

G. endressii ●◑○

Herbaceous perennial · Medium · All summer · Zones 4–8

Bigger and more aggressive, this species has fresh, pale green leaves and silvery pink flowers (most silvery in the form 'A.T. Johnson'), for a long season, except for hot regions where it flowers only in early summer. Useful in shade, even dry shade.

G. macrorrhizum ●◑○

Herbaceous perennial · Medium · Early summer · Evergreen· Zones 3–8

Very useful plant which will do well even in dry shade. Round, scalloped aromatic leaves which colour well in autumn and pink flowers. A single plant can readily be split into several pieces, by pulling apart its brown papery stems and roots.

G. sanguineum ◑○

Rock plant · Medium · Summer · Evergreen · Zones 3–9

There are various cultivars of this low, mound-forming species, in colours ranging from white through pink to strong magenta. All have finely cut leaves and open flowers and are best in sun.

G. wallichianum 'Buxton's Variety' ◑○

Herbaceous perennial · Medium · Late summer · Zones 6–9

Marvellous spreading plant with blue flowers with white centres and dark stamens on trailing stems. Collect seed as soon as it ripens (the plant does not hold it for long), and sow immediately to propagate this delightful and useful variety.

Gypsophila paniculata 'Rosy Veil' ○

Herbaceous perennial · Medium · Late summer · Zones 3–9

Usefully late-flowering plant for a sunny, well-drained position; above narrow glaucous leaves appear clouds of tiny pink double flowers. A lovely, delicate thing.

G. repens 'Dorothy Teacher' ○

Rock plant · Small · Summer · Evergreen · Zones 3–8

A smaller, cushion-forming plant with single pink flowers held close to the grey-blue leaves. Pretty on a low, sunny wall.

Hedera helix (IVY) ●◑○

Self-clinging creeper · Variable · Foliage · Evergreen · Zones 5–9

There are several dwarf or miniature cultivars of the common ivy which are useful on a shady wall, but often these are less hardy depending on variety. 'Arran' is a plain green type; 'Jubilee' has rather pear-shaped leaves with cream variegation; 'Petit Point' has trident-shaped green leaves. Specialist growers can advise on the hardiness of their varieties.

Helianthemum nummularium ○
(ROCK ROSE)

Rock plant · Low, spreading · Summer · Evergreen · Zones 7–9

The rock roses are plants for full sun: the papery flowers will not open in shade. There are single and double forms, in colours ranging from pale pink and yellow through to hot shades of red and orange, and the foliage is green or grey. Use them to make intermingling patches of colour and allow them enough space – each plant could easily cover a square yard in warmer zones. Clip after flowering to keep them neat.

Helleborus foetidus ●◑○
(STINKING HELLEBORE)

Herbaceous perennial · Medium · Winter to spring · Evergreen · Zones 6–9

Plant normally associated with a shady border, but seedlings quite frequently appear in loose stonework and appear to thrive, even in full sun. The handsome, dark, long-fingered leaves are a permanent asset, and the clusters of pale apple-green flowers, sometimes with purple edges to the petals, last for literally months. A plant to encourage.

Iberis sempervirens 'Snowflake' ◑○
(CANDYTUFT)

Rock plant · Small · Spring · Evergreen · Zones 3–9

Good evergreen mound which is attractive throughout the year. In spring the chalk-white flowers cover the plant. Clip over after flowering.

Lavandula angustifolia ○
(LAVENDER)

Shrub · Medium to large · Summer · Evergreen · Zones 6–10

Old English lavender is a familiar aromatic shrub which revels in poor soil, full sun and good drainage. There are white and pale pink varieties, as well as the usual pale purple shade, but these are somehow less satisfactory. 'Hidcote' is a useful compact variety, with especially dark flowers. Clip over after flowering, removing about an inch of the foliage to keep the plant neat; lavender does not regrow from old wood.

Lespedeza thunbergii ◑○
(BUSH CLOVER)
Shrub · Large · Late summer/autumn · Zones 5–9

Late to leaf and flower, but when it does, it makes a graceful plant with arching slender stems and extended panicles of rose-purple flowers. Good to soften the top of a large sunny wall. More vigorous in warm regions.

Linaria purpurea 'Canon Went' ◑○
(TOADFLAX)
Herbaceous perennial · Tall · Summer · Zones 4–10

Many toadflaxes will be happy on or in a wall; this one has tall narrow spikes of pale pink flowers and will seed itself into tiny cracks. A proper cottage plant with no bad habits – unwanted seedlings are easily removed.

Lithodora diffusa ○
Rock plant · Low, spreading · Summer · Evergreen · Zones 6–9

Best on lime-free soil, such as sandy peat, and in full sun, this low-growing evergreen shrub bears beautiful sky-blue flowers over a long season. The variety 'Heavenly Blue' is the bluest and best kind.

Lysimachia nummularia 'Aurea' ◑
(CREEPING JENNY)
Groundcover · Low, spreading · Foliage · Evergreen · Zones 3–9

The golden-leaved creeping Jenny is a lovely bright thing for part shade and a dampish soil.

The colour of the foliage is reinforced in summer by the single yellow flowers.

Meconopsis cambrica (WELSH POPPY)
Biennial · Medium · Early summer · Zones 6–9 ●◑○

This will certainly seed itself once you have introduced a plant into the garden, and some people regard it as a weed, but the ferny leaves are such a fresh green and the delicate flowers are so appealing in shades of yellow and pale orange that I welcome each new generation. Set at the base of a wall, in sun or shade, and wait for it to spread into the wall itself. The only *Meconopsis* to survive heat and humidity.

Oenothera missouriensis ○
(MISSOURI PRIMROSE)
Herbaceous perennial · Medium · Summer to autumn · Zones 4–9

A prostrate evening primrose with shiny green narrow leaves on lax, crimson stems. The large yellow flowers may be 10cm (4in) across and they have a long season. Full sun and good drainage.

Omphalodes verna (BLUE-EYED MARY) ●
Rock plant · Small · Spring · Zones 5–9

Good plant for moisture-retentive soil in shade, where it will make a dense clump of heart-shaped leaves; the blue flowers look like forget-me-nots.

Perovskia atriplicifolia (RUSSIAN SAGE) ○
Shrub · Large · Late summer · Zones 5–9

Although technically a shrub, this is generally cut to the ground over winter. It sends up pale felted stems decorated with deeply cut grey

green leaves, and by late summer the entire plant is dominated by the airy, stiff panicles of lavender-blue flowers. 'Blue Haze' is a good named variety. Well-drained soil, full sun.

Phlox 'Chattahoochee' ◑
Rock plant · Medium · Spring · Zones 6–9

A lovely plant which may be tricky to grow well. Give it a partly shaded position and make sure the soil does not dry out. It will reward the right treatment with a long display of its blue, pinky-red centred flowers. The foliage is dark green and the stems tend to trail in a lax manner. Propagate from cuttings every few years to replace old plants.

P. douglasii ◑○
Rock plant · Small, spreading · Spring · Evergreen · Zones 6–9

Good carpet-formers, well able to resist drought. Masses of flowers: 'Daniel's Cushion' has large rose pink blooms; 'May Snow' is pure white, and there are several others.

P. stolonifera ●◑
Groundcover · Small, spreading · Spring · Zones 2–8

An indispensable creeping groundcover for shade above or below a wall. Flower colour ranges from white to pink and purple depending on variety. 'Sharwood Purple' is a particularly strong-growing type.

P. subulata ◑○
Rock plant · Small, spreading · Early spring · Evergreen · Zones 2–9

Varieties of this species make a less dense mat of foliage. 'Oakington Blue', 'Scarlet Flame' and 'White Delight' are all good examples.

Polygonum affine ◐○

Herbaceous perennial · Medium · Summer to autumn · Zones 6–9

Carpeting plant with none of the dangerously invasive tendencies of some larger members of the knotweed family, although it does spread. The leaves turn from green to foxy brown in autumn and persist through the winter; the pink spikes of flowers deepen with age. 'Superbum' is the variety to look out for, or else 'Lowndes Variety', which has salmon pink double flowers and is less vigorous.

P. capitatum (KNOTWEED)

Rock plant · Small, spreading · Summer · Zones 9–11

Not as hardy as the two species below, but a pretty spreader for a sunny position. The rounded dull green leaves are attractively marked with reddish brown, and the pink flower heads are rounded.

P. vaccinifolium

Rock plant · Small · Autumn · Zones 7–9

A miniature species for lime-free soil. It grows close to the ground and makes a dense mat of warm brown stems, decorated with tiny glossy green leaves. The pink flowers are also tiny, but freely produced.

Pulmonaria (LUNGWORT) ◕◑

Herbaceous perennial · Small/Medium · Spring · Evergreen · Zones 2–9

The lungworts are a valuable group of plants with good foliage, often blotched with white or silver, bearing welcome spring flowers. All the kinds listed below like moisture-retentive soil and at least partial shade, although they will put up a fair display even where it is dry.

P. angustifolia

Zones 2–9

'Munstead Variety' is a small, early, very blue lungwort, with unmarked leaves and a tidy habit.

P. rubra 'Redstart'

Zones 3–9

A larger lungwort, with soft green unspotted leaves throughout the year and pinky-red flowers for several months from early spring.

P. saccharata

Zones 3–9

There are several named forms of this species, which are characterised by the silvery marbling on the leaves. 'Highdown' is a good blue; 'Margery Fish' has particularly well-marked foliage and pink and blue flowers; 'Alba' has clear white flowers.

Rosmarinus lavandulaceus

Shrub · Small, spreading · Spring onwards · Evergreen · Zones 9–10

A lovely thing for a hot retaining wall, where this prostrate, very small-leaved rosemary can sprawl and spread. Its flowers are an intense blue.

R. officinalis (ROSEMARY) ○

Shrub · Large · Spring onwards · Evergreen · Zones 8–10

Rosemary can make a wonderfully gnarled shape if it is planted at the top of a sunny wall and allowed to grow without interference. The narrow dark leaves are paler beneath and pungently aromatic, and the pale blue flowers appear early in the year and are never absent for long. 'Severn Sea' has arching branches which are particularly picturesque, but it is a less hardy variety. 'Arp' (zone 7) is the hardiest variety.

Saxifraga ●◐

Rock plant · Small · Spring to autumn · Evergreen · Zones 2–7 depending on variety

There are masses of these attractive plants which are usually found on a rock garden, but they are useful too on or in a retaining wall. The encrusted types, such as *S. paniculata* 'Lutea' need good drainage and full sun, the kabschia types need well-drained soil but some shade, whilst the mossy types like a moister soil, again in semi-shade. *S. × urbium* (zones 6–7), better known as London Pride, makes a good show of delicate pink flowers over glossy green rosettes of foliage in late spring. Try it in the shade. Most saxifrages are sensitive to excessive summer heat.

Sedum acre ◐○

Rock plant · Small · Summer · Evergreen · Zones 3–8

Small plant, which can become invasive, but is very valuable to soften new stonework. Tiny succulent leaves of fresh green quickly make an enlarging mat; the starry yellow flowers appear in summer. The new spring growth of 'Aureum' is warm yellow. Other good sedums, all with succulent leaves and needing full sun, are *S. spathulifolium* (zones 5–9) with fleshy purple rosettes and yellow flowers, and varieties of *S. spurium* (zones 3–8). A good nursery will supply these and many more.

Sempervivum (HOUSE LEEK) ◑○
Rock plant · Small/medium · Foliage · Evergreen · Zones
4–9 depending on variety

Large group of plants with unusual succulent
leaves arranged in rosettes. They range from
tiny to much larger, and many have interesting and beautiful colour combinations, as well
as textures varying from cobwebbed to waxen.
All grow slowly, by making new rosettes
adjacent to the original, and they need full
sun. But some can grow practically on bare
stone, nourished only by rainfall. Not for
those who want instant effects, but worthwhile none the less.

Thymus (THYME) ○
Groundcover · Small · Summer · Evergreen · Zones 3–9
depending on variety

Culinary herbs which like sun and good
drainage. Useful where space is limited. Bees
like the small flowers.

T. citriodorus 'Silver Queen'
Zones 6–9

Lemon-scented thyme with pretty variegated
leaves, grey-green and silver. Makes an attractive miniature bush up to a foot high and
needs full sun and good drainage.

T. 'Doone Valley'
Zones 3–7

Good spreading variety, making a carpet of
dark green foliage marked and speckled with
gold. Large heads of mauve flowers in late
summer.

T. serpyllum
Zones 3–9

The creeping thyme; there are various named
varieties: 'Albus' is white, 'Coccineus' rich
crimson, and 'Pink Chintz' a particularly pretty pale pink.

Viola ◑○
Rock plant · Small · Spring to autumn · Evergreen · Zones
6–9

A large group of plants, most of which appreci-
ate some shade and moisture-retentive soil.
Varieties of *V. cornuta* (zones 6–10) are particularly useful, for their long season and the attractive manner in which the flower stems insinuate
themselves among other plants. There are so
many cultivated forms of small pansy (violas
and violettas), that it is hard to pinpoint just
one or two: 'Hunterscombe Purple' has large,
richly coloured flowers and is very reliable;
'Maggie Mott' has even larger flowers of lavender blue with yellow centres; 'Moonlight' has
small, fragrant creamy yellow flowers. All do
best if deadheaded periodically, and fed to
encourage more flowers. They suffer during
excessive summer heat. 'Princess Blue' is a particularly heat-tolerant form blooming throughout the summer.

HEDGES

As explained in the main Hedge section
(pp.102–113), hedges may be either formal or
informal: either tightly clipped or allowed to
grow (and probably flower), in a more natural
fashion. But although hedges may be so catego-
rized, it is not so easy to place the plants of
which they may be composed rigidly in one or
other category. Some, such as certain kinds of

cotoneaster, can be treated rigidly or else
allowed free rein; others, such as Hidcote
lavender, have a formal feel even though they
flower, simply because of the plant's habit.
Furthermore, it would be impossible to make an
exhaustive list of hedging plants, because practically any shrub or tree could be used. The
selection below, then, includes recognized formal hedging plants together with a personal
selection from the myriad shrubs which can be
used informally. Planting distances are of
course approximate; set plants closer if you
want a low, dense hedge quickly, but allow
more space if the hedge is intended to be particularly tall. Heights are given to provide a
rough idea of the tallest hedge a given plant
could make.

Plants for formal hedges

Buxus sempervirens (BOX) ◑○
Evergreen · 2.5m (8ft) or 60cm (2ft) · Zones 5–9

The common box makes a good dense
hedge with its small dark green leaves.
'Handsworthensis' is the best kind for a tall
hedge, whilst 'Suffruticosa' (zones 6–9) is the
dwarf variety used for edgings. Needs several
clippings a year to keep it looking neat, which
is the *sine qua non* of dwarf box, at least.
Planting distances depend on variety:
15–60cm (6–24in).

Carpinus betulus (HORNBEAM) ◑○
Deciduous · 6m (20ft) · Zones 4–7

Hornbeam looks superficially like beech, but
its pleated leaves are rougher and more pointed, and in winter they are not so warm a
brown (they remain on the plant over winter if

the clipping is done late in the summer). A good hardy hedge, slowish but worth the wait. Plant 60cm (2ft) apart.

Cotoneaster ◑○
Deciduous or semi-evergreen · 2.5m (8ft) · Zones 6–10

C. salicifolius var. *floccosus* (zones 6–9) is an upright form with smallish, deep green semi-evergreen leaves and clusters of red fruits that last into the new year. Plant up to 2m (6ft) apart for a loose hedge 1.5–2m (5–6ft) high.

Crataegus phaenopyrum ◑○
(WASHINGTON HAWTHORN)
Deciduous · 3.5m (12ft) · Zones 3–8

This is one of the most commonly planted small trees in the eastern US because of its tough constitution and quick growth. The new leaves open a most refreshing shade of pale green, and a hedge which is not too hard clipped will bear cream flowers in early summer and red berries (haws) in autumn. The foliage colours well before falling. A good hedge. Plant 30–60cm (1–2ft) apart.

Fagus sylvatica (BEECH) ◑○
Deciduous, retains old leaves · 6m (20ft) · Zones 4–7

Beech is a large forest tree and can make a very tall hedge, supposing one has the equipment to clip such a feature; it will also make a more modest hedge, up to 2–2.5m (6–8ft). The foxy brown leaves make a warm screen in winter, but it is a dominating colour and not the best background to a spring planting of, say, hellebores. The new leaves burst out as a great relief, pale silky green darkening and thickening with age. Slow, but only requiring a single clip each year. Plant 45–90cm (18–36in) apart.

Griselinia littoralis ◑○
Evergreen · 2m (6ft) · Zones 9–10

A good seaside hedge, because its shiny, soapy-textured leaves resist salt spray, but less hardy inland. The foliage is a distinct apple green, although there are variegated kinds which are useful where the hedge is to stand alone. Plant 2.5m (8ft) apart.

Ilex (HOLLY) ◑○
Evergreen · Zones 6–9

Holly makes an extremely good and impenetrable hedge, with its tough, usually spiny, foliage. Berries will only be borne by female plants, and then only if they are not close-clipped and if there is a male plant close by to pollinate the flowers.

I. crenata (JAPANESE HOLLY) ◑○
Variable height · Evergreen · Zones 5–8

One of the most popular landscape plants in the USA where hardy, but not well adapted to the deep south. Small leaves resemble box in size, but the plant habit is much stiffer and it is hardier. Black berries in autumn are not a particularly attractive feature. There are many varieties of appropriate size for the desired hedge. 'Helleri' is low and mounded and makes a good edging hedge. Particularly good in zone 8. 'Convexa' is well suited to a medium-sized hedge 120–150cm (4–5ft) high. 'Microphylla' has smaller leaves but a taller almost tree-like habit ideal for tall hedges 2m (6ft) or more tall.

I. opaca (AMERICAN HOLLY) ◑○
15m (50ft) · Evergreen · Zones 5–9

Vigorous and hardy native of eastern North America, but it does not do so well in the Pacific north-west. Makes an excellent large hedge. Female plants bear attractive fruit. There are numerous varieties: 'Canary' bears yellow berries which are especially attractive when planted with red-fruited varieties. 'Old Heavy Berry' and 'Jersey Princess' have deep green leaves and red berries. 'Steward's Silver Crown' is one of the best of a very few variegated varieties. White-edged leaves and red berries.

I. × messerveae (BLUE HOLLY) ◑○
3–4.5m (10–15ft) · Evergreen · Zones 4–9

These relatively new hybrids of the tender English holly have become the most popular and reliable of all hollies today. Bluish-green glossy foliage with bright red fruit. 'Blue Princess' and 'Blue Prince' are extremely hardy with compact growth. 'Golden Girl' has yellow fruit.

Laurus nobilis (BAY LAUREL) ○
Evergreen · 6m (20ft) · Zones 8–10

In colder areas, bay needs the protection of a warm wall, but in mild coastal regions it makes an excellent hedge. The leathery aromatic leaves make a dense mosaic. Plant 60cm (2ft) apart.

Ligustrum ovalifolium ◑○
(OVAL LEAF PRIVET)
Semi-evergreen · 3m (10ft) · Zones 5–9

A common hedge, but not one of the best. It grows quickly, but needs frequent trimming to keep it neat, and its greedy roots spread widely, leaving the soil dry and poor. The golden form, 'Aureum', is pleasantly bright, showing the best colour in sun. The leaves are lost in particularly cold weather. Plant 45cm (18in) apart. *L. amurense*, the Amur privet (zones 3–7), is equally undistinguished, but useful in colder climates.

Lonicera nitida
(BOXLEAF HONEYSUCKLE) ◐○
Evergreen · 120cm (4ft) · Zones 7–9

This shrubby honeysuckle with its tiny leaves makes a reasonable small hedge, but its brittle twigs are easily damaged. A heavy snowfall, for instance, can be disastrous. Not an easy hedge to renovate; if it does become misshapen it is best to start afresh and replant. Plant 30cm (1ft) apart.

Prunus cerasifera ◐○
(MYROBALAN PLUM)
Deciduous · 2.5m (8ft) · Zones 3–8

A good rural hedge, with its mass of tiny white flowers early in spring and small, edible cherry plums in autumn. It can grow tall without taking much horizontal space. The variety 'Pissardii' has purple foliage which deepens from translucent dark red in spring. The early flowers open white from pink buds. Plant 45–60cm (18–24in) apart.

P. lusitanica (PORTUGUESE LAUREL)
Evergreen · 3.5m (12ft) · Zones 8–10 ●◐○

Makes a good big hedge, with dark leaves rather like those of the bay, but with distinctive red petioles. A useful plant on limy or chalk soils. Plant at least 60 cm (2ft) apart for a tall hedge.

P. spinosa (BLACKTHORN) ◐○
Deciduous · 2.5m (8ft) · Zones 4–8

A traditional rural hedge in Britain; its mass of white flowers appears on black twigs early in the year and often heralds a cold snap: 'blackthorn winter'. Later, there are dull green leaves, which may be further decorated in autumn with small black fruits. These sloes, with their plummy bloom and dry, unbearably bitter taste, are nevertheless essential ingredients in the old winter warmer, sloe gin. Plant 30–60cm (1–2ft) apart.

Taxus baccata (ENGLISH YEW) ◐○
Evergreen · 6m (20ft) · Zones 6–7

Undoubtedly the king of hedges, apart from the fact that it must never be used where livestock might reach and eat it – its leaves contain a deadly poison which remains potent even in withered clippings. Its matt green foliage makes the ideal background to plain lawns as well as a bright flower border, and older hedges can survive drastic pruning to keep them within bounds. It can grow 30cm (1ft) a year if properly planted and fed. Equally good on acid or alkaline soil. Plant 60cm (2ft) apart, more for a really high hedge. 'Elegantissima' is a golden type which makes a good, dense hedge. *T. × media* is hardier. Several upright forms such as 'Hicksii' make excellent hedges (zones 4–7).

Thuja plicata ◐○
(WESTERN RED CEDAR)
Evergreen · 4.5m (15ft) · Zones 5–7

Makes a good tight hedge, but it lacks the refinement of yew. It is faster, making perhaps 60cm (2ft) a year, so it needs clipping at least twice every growing season. Pleasantly

aromatic foliage and the hedge can be kept narrow. Tolerates chalk soils. Plant 60–90cm (2–3ft) apart. *T. occidentalis*, the eastern arborvitae (zones 2–8) is hardier and less vigorous. Foliage is often pale green in winter, so choose a deep green variety such as 'Nigra' which does not fade.

Informal hedges

Berberis × stenophylla ◐○
Evergreen · 2–2.5m (6–8ft) · Zones 7–9

A rather formless plant which has long drooping branches, small dark leaves and extremely bright egg-yellow flowers in late spring. Not my favourite, but a reliable performer in all well-drained soils; also withstands salt winds. Plant 90–150cm (3–5ft) apart.

B. thunbergii ◐○
Deciduous · 90–150cm (3–5ft) · Zones 4–8

Useful for a small hedge. Good red berries and bright autumn foliage. There are several forms with coloured and variegated foliage which can be incorporated into a special colour scheme. Plant 30–60cm (1–2ft) apart.

Buddleia davidii ○
(BUTTERFLY BUSH)
Deciduous · 2–3m (6–10ft) · Zones 5–9 (herbaceous in Zone 5)

Makes a striking hedge for late summer, when the long racemes of scented flowers will attract flocks of butterflies. There are several named forms, ranging in colour from white through pale mauve to strong purple; the whites I find unattractive because they contrast unpleasantly with the brown, faded blooms. Prune hard in spring. Only suitable for a large garden, because the hedge looks brutalised after pruning. Sunny, well-drained position. Plant 120cm–2m (4–6ft) apart.

Chaenomeles (JAPANESE QUINCE) ◑○
Deciduous · 1–2m (4–6ft) · Zones 6–9

See Shrub section above. Plant at least 90 cm (3ft) apart.

Cornus alba (DOGWOOD) ◑◑
Deciduous · 2–2.5m (6–8ft) · Zones 2–8

The red-barked dogwood is marvellous for damper parts of a garden (although it is not restricted to such sites), where it can be pruned to make a screen. The red colour is most intense on new shoots, so plants should be pollarded every other year to encourage these. 'Elegantissima' is attractive in summer too, because of its variegated leaves, margined irregularly with white. Plant 120cm–2m (4–6ft) apart.

Escallonia ◑○
Evergreen · 2–2.5m (6–8ft) · Zones 7 or 8–9

Good plants for mild coastal areas, with their small shiny salt-resistant leaves. Also tolerant of lime and drought, but less reliable inland. There are many named varieties, most with pink or red flowers in late summer and autumn. The species *E. iveyi* has larger leaves and correspondingly larger panicles of white flowers. Plant 90–150cm (3–5ft) apart.

Fuchsia ◑○
Deciduous · 90–180cm (3–6ft) · Zones 8–10

Only suitable for hedging in mild areas; elsewhere, cold weather will cut the plants to the ground each winter. There are numerous varieties, all very floriferous and colourful. *F. magellanica* (root-hardy in zone 6 with a mulch) is the hardiest and is pretty because its flowers are slender, lacking the bulk which sometimes spoils the larger varieties; there is a particularly attractive form, 'Versicolor'. This has greyish leaves with pink tints when young and marked with cream when they mature. Plant 60–120cm (2–4ft) apart.

Lavandula angustifolia ○
(OLD ENGLISH LAVENDER)
Evergreen · 60–90cm (2–3ft) · Zones 6–10

See section on Plants for Retaining Walls. Set 2.75–3.5m (9–12ft) apart.

Potentilla fruticosa ○
Deciduous · 60–120 cm (2–4ft) · Zones 6–9

There are many varieties and a number make good small hedges. They flower practically all summer and the warm brown stems are not unattractive during the winter. 'Elizabeth' is a good variety, with rich yellow flowers; 'Primrose Beauty' has paler flowers and grey foliage on arching branches. Hotter colours are found in 'Red Ace' and 'Tangerine'. There are white forms, but these are generally less satisfactory. Plant 30–60cm (1–2ft) apart.

Rosa ◑○
Deciduous · 90cm-3m (3–10ft) · Zones 2–10 depending on variety

One could make a hedge with practically any of the shrub roses, so the choice here is enormously wide but disease resistance should be a major consideration. The Japanese rugosas (zones 2–7) grow on poor soil, need little attention and most offer flowers and fruit, as well as good autumn colour. The modern shrub 'Nevada' makes a well-clothed bush absolutely covered with large, single, pale yellow flowers in summer, with sporadic blooms later. In a smaller space, try the suckering Scotch rose, *R. pimpinellifolia*. The hybrid musk roses, which include 'Buff Beauty', 'Moonlight' and the pink 'Felicia', make a wider hedge, because of their more spreading habit. The main flowering season is in summer, but if you deadhead them there will be a welcome repeat performance in October. They are healthy plants with strongly-scented flowers. Plant a rose hedge according to the variety chosen, at a distance a little less than you expect each individual rose to spread.

The new landscape roses are highly disease-resistant, requiring virtually no spraying to remain attractive and they bloom continuously. 'Bonica' has pink flowers followed by red hips in autumn. 'Pink Meidland' is pink with a white centre. Both make hedges about 120cm (4ft) high and should be planted about 90cm (3ft) apart (zones 3–10).

Rosmarinus officinalis (ROSEMARY) ○
Evergreen · 90–150cm (3–5ft) · Zones 7–10

See Plants for Retaining Walls (p.137). Makes a quirky hedge, since each plant will bulge and billow as it wishes, unless you choose the more upright 'Miss Jessop's Variety'. Plant 60cm (2ft) apart.

Salix alba ◑○
Deciduous · 2–2.5m (6–8ft) · Zones 3–9

Like the dogwood mentioned above, a plant to coppice for the sake of its bright winter twigs. 'Britzensis' has orange-scarlet stems; 'Vitellina's' are egg yellow. The violet willow, *S. daphnoides* has purple shoots covered with pale bloom. For an informal screen in a damp corner. Plant 90–120cm (3–4ft) apart.

• PLANTS BY SITE •

These may provide a starting point when planning a garden. More information, which may qualify the bald classifications made here, is to be found in the Plant Reference section (pp. 114–141). Genus names refer only to the species described in the book.

UNFUSSY PLANTS

(those which have no particular need for extra warmth and which thrive in a mixture of sun and shade in ordinary garden soil).

CLIMBERS

Aristolochia
Celastrus
Clematis (many, see other lists for those requiring special conditions)
Eccremocarpus
Humulus
Lathyrus
Parthenocissus
Roses (see later list for shade-tolerant varieties)
Vitis coignetiae
Wisteria

SHRUBS

Ceratostigma
Chaenomeles
Choisya
Cotoneaster
Euonymus
Forsythia
Kerria
Pyracantha

FRUIT

Apples, many varieties
Plums and damsons

PLANTS FOR RETAINING WALLS

Alchemilla
Anemone
Campanula
Centranthus
Corydalis
Digitalis
Erigeron
Erinus
Geranium
Meconopsis
Polygonum (not *vaccinifolium*)

PLANTS WHICH NEED A WARM WALL

CLIMBERS

Actinidia
Campsis
Clematis armandii
C. cirrhosa balearica
Jasminum affine
Passiflora
Rhodochiton
Rosa banksiae
R. laevigata
Schizophragma
Solanum
Trachelospermum
Vitis (most)

SHRUBS

Abelia
Abutilon
Acacia
Akebia
Buddleia
Carpenteria
Ceanothus
Chimonanthus
Colutea
Convolvulus
Cytisus
Lagerstroemeria
Laurus
Lavatera
Lippia
Magnolia grandiflora
Myrtus
Phygelius
Piptanthus
Pittosporum
Teucrium

FRUIT

Apricots, nectarines and peaches
Cherries, sweet
Fig
Grapevine
Pear

PLANTS FOR RETAINING WALLS

Acaena
*Alyssum**
*Anthemis**
*Arabis**

Aubrieta
*Cerastium**
Cistus
Cytisus
*Dianthus**
*Euphorbia myrsinites**
Genista
Gypsophila
*Helianthemum**
*Iberis**
Lespedeza
Lavandula
Oenothera
Perovskia
Phlox
Rosmarinus
Saxifraga (aizoon)
Sedum
Sempervivum
Thymus

*Very hardy alpines which need sunlight rather than warmth

PLANTS HAPPY IN SHADE
(many of these are also happy in some sun or even a completely sunny position: those which cannot tolerate heat are mentioned)

CLIMBERS
Clematis — many, including *C. alpina, campaniflora, × jackmanii, macropetala, montana,* 'Comtesse de Bouchard', 'Henryi', 'Joan Picton', 'Marie Boisselot', 'Perle d'Azur', 'The President', 'Wada's Primrose' and 'William Kennett'. Of these, only 'Wada's Primrose' must be kept out of the sun.
Hedera
Lonicera — keep from hot sun, except *L. sempervirens*
Pileostegia

Roses — many, including *R. × anemonoides,* 'Albéric Barbier', 'Bobbie James', 'Emily Gray', 'Félicité et Perpétue', 'François Juranville', 'Goldfinch', 'Lawrence Johnston', 'Leverkusen', Mermaid', 'Mme Alfred Carrière', 'Mme Grégoire Staechelin', 'New Dawn' and 'Zéphirine Drouhin'.

SHRUBS
Choisya
Cotoneaster
Hydrangea
Jasminum nudiflorum
Pyracantha
Viburnum
Taxus

FRUIT
Cherry, morello
Currants, red and white
Gooseberry

PLANTS FOR RETAINING WALLS
Adiantum (not sun)
Ajuga
Anemone
Asplenium
Athyrium (not sun)
Blechnum (not sun)
Cotyledon
Digitalis
Dryopteris (not sun)
Euphorbia robbiae
Geranium endressii
G. macrorrhizum
Hedera
Helleborus
Lysimachia
Omphalodes (not sun)
Pulmonaria (not sun)

Saxifraga umbrosa, and *Kabschia* and mossy types
Viola

PLANTS WHICH TOLERATE CHALK

CLIMBERS
Clematis
Lonicera
Solanum

SHRUBS
Buddleia
Colutea
Forsythia
Kerria
Laurus
Pyracantha
Rosmarinus

PLANTS FOR RETAINING WALLS
Aspleniun
Cistus
Gypsophila
Lavandula
Helianthemum
Perovskia

HEDGES
Berberis
Carpinus
Crataegus
Fagus
Lavandula
Ligustrum
Lonicera
Potentilla
Prunus
Rosmarinus
Taxus
Thuja

PLANTS INTOLERANT OF ALKALINE SOILS

CLIMBERS
Tropaeolum speciosum

SHRUBS
Acacia
Camellia

PLANTS FOR RETAINING WALLS
Lithodora
Polygonum vaccinifolium

PLANTS SUITABLE FOR CLAY SOILS

CLIMBERS
Actinidia
Aristolochia
Clematis
Hedera *
Humulus
Hydrangea
Jasminum
Lonicera
Parthenocissus
Passiflora
Pileostegia
Polygonum *
Rosa
Schizophragma
Solanum
Trachelospermum
Vitis
Wisteria

SHRUBS
Abelia
Buddleia
Chaenomeles

Choisya
Colutea
Cotoneaster
Cytisus
Euonymus
Forsythia
Garrya
Genista
Hydrangea
Jasminum
Kerria
Laurus
Magnolia
Myrtus
Pittosporum
Pyracantha
Viburnum

PLANTS FOR RETAINING WALLS
Alchemilla
Anemone
Euphorbia robbiae
Geranium
*Hedera**
Helleborus

HEDGES
Berberis
Buxus
Carpinus
Cornus
*Crataegus**
Ilex
Ligustrum
Lonicera
Potentilla
Prunus
*Salix**
Sorbus
Taxus

Thuja
Tilia

*Those which tolerate very heavy clay

EVERGREENS

CLIMBERS
Clematis armandii
Hedera
Pileostegia
Trachelospermum

SHRUBS
Abelia
Acacia
Camellia
Carpenteria
Ceanothus (some)
Choisya
Convolvulus
Coronilla
Cotoneaster (some)
Fremontodendron
Garrya
Laurus
Magnolia grandiflora
Myrtus
Piptanthus
Pittosporum
Pyracantha
Teucrium

PLANTS FOR RETAINING WALLS
Acaena
Ajuga
Alyssum
Anthemis
Arabis
Asplenium

Aubrieta
Blechnum
Campanulua
Ceanothus
Cerastium
Cistus
Cotyledon
Dianthus
Erinus
Erysimum
Euphorbia
Geranium
Gypsophila repens
Hedera
Helianthemum
Helleborus
Iberis
Lavandula
Lithodora
Lysimachia
Omphalodes
Phlox
Pulmonaria
Rosmarinus
Saxifraga
Sedum
Sempervivum
Thymus
Viola

HEDGES
Berberis (some)
Buxus
Cotoneaster (some)
Escallonia
Griselinia
Ilex
Lavandula
Ligustrum
Lonicera
Prunus lusitanica

Rosmarinus
Taxus
Thuja

WINTER AND EARLY SPRING FLOWERS

CLIMBERS
Clematis armandii
C. cirrhosa balearica

SHRUBS
Acacia
Camellia
Chaenomeles
Chimonanthus
Coronilla
Forsythia
Garrya

PLANTS FOR RETAINING WALLS
Alyssum
Aubrieta
Erysimum
Euphorbia
Helleborus
Iberis
Omphalodes
Pulmonaria
Rosmarinus

QUICK SPREADERS

CLIMBERS
Aristolochia
Celastrus
Clematis montana
C. orientalis
Cobaea
Humulus
Lonicera

Parthenocissus
Polygonum
Roses (most)
Solanum
Vitis
Wisteria

SHRUBS
Abutilon
Acacia
Buddleia
Ceanothus
Cytisus
Lavatera

PLANTS FOR RETAINING WALLS
Acaena
Alchemilla (self-seeder)
Anthemis
Ceanothus
Centranthus (self-seeder)
Erigeron (self-seeder)
Euphorbia robbiae
Helianthemum
Meconopsis (self-seeder)
Polygonum

• PRUNING •

There is a lot of unnecessary mystique attached to the subject of pruning. Some wall plants need little or no attention — self-clingers such as ivy and Virginia creeper, and naturally well-formed shrubs such as *Magnolia* and *Carpenteria* — but the majority of plants we choose to grow by a wall or fence need regular pruning. In the instructions below, I have tried to explain general principles rather than dictate absolutes, so that you understand the process and can bend the rules to suit each individual plant and your own preferences. The one universal rule is that dead, damaged and diseased wood (the three D's), should be removed, and one should always begin by doing this. Thereafter, each pruning cut must be justified: if in doubt, leave a branch rather than remove it.

A really good pair of secateurs (hand pruners) is essential. These will be expensive but it is not worth economizing on quality. For renovating older plants, long-handled loppers and perhaps a small saw will be needed. Where a large proportion of the plant is being removed, such as when you prune some roses and certain clematis varieties, remember to feed well: apply a good dressing of rotted manure or compost and water well if the weather is dry so that the plant can quickly recover.

Some climbers need no pruning except to keep them within bounds. These include *Actinidia kolomikta, Akebia, Aristolochia, Celastrus, Hedera* species and varieties thereof,

Hydrangea, Jasminum officinale, Parthenocissus, Pileostegia and ornamental *Vitis*, except if you want to make them into formal shapes. Note that *Vitis* should be pruned before Christmas; after that the sap begins to rise and the wounds will weep copiously.

Flowering climbers can be approached with one simple rule in mind: those that flower early in the year on wood produced the previous season should be pruned soon after flowering, whereas those that flower after midsummer on wood produced during the current season should be pruned in late winter or early spring.

Some vigorous plants, such as *Wisteria*, need summer pruning too (see below for details); by cutting back the long shoots, food is channelled into making flower buds and flowering spurs are thus produced.

Clematis

Although there are so many kinds of clematis, they can be divided into four categories for the purposes of pruning, so there is no need to be daunted by the group as a whole. All clematis should be pruned after planting, whatever time of year this is done, to about 30cm (1ft) from the base. Cut each stem above a strong-looking pair of buds. This encourages the plant to form several stems and to become more bushy.

Later pruning depends on flowering time:

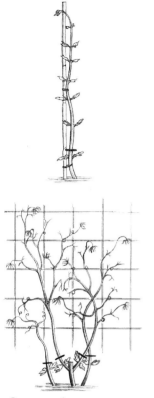

Summer and autumn-flowering clematis

Top: After planting, reduce the plant to about 30cm (1ft), cutting above a good pair of buds.

Bottom: In succeeding years the whole plant is cut back close to ground level in early spring. Be careful to cut above the lowest pair of strong, promising buds on each stem. The exceptions to the rule are the late-flowering species C. *orientalis* and *tangutica* which can be left unpruned.

1. Those that flower in summer and autumn on the current season's growths. These include many large-flowered hybrids such as 'Comtesse de Bouchard', 'Ernest Markham', 'Huldine' and 'Perle d'Azur', as well as the species C. *campaniflora, flammula, jackmanii, jouiniana* 'Praecox', *rhederiana, texensis* and *viticella*.

   Prune at planting. In subsequent years, simply cut right back almost to ground level during winter or early spring, making the cuts just above the lowest pair of strong buds on each stem.

   The exceptions to this rule are those vigorous late-flowering species C. *orientalis* and *tangutica*, which can be left unpruned to make a large mass. They can be cut back to the main framework in spring if you like, or indeed cut right back if you need to keep them within bounds.

2. The spring-flowering species which flower on growth produced the previous summer. These include C. *alpina, macropetala* and *montana*. In many situations these will need no pruning once they are established, but it is worth taking some trouble to establish a firm framework in the first couple of years. Prune at planting and, the following winter, cut back the new shoots by one half. Train the new growth during the following summer and prune any laterals which have flowered to one or two buds from the main framework. Thereafter, the rampant C. *montana* can be left alone: you might want to clip it over after flowering where you can reach it, but this is not necessary. With the smaller species, flowered shoots can

be pruned straight after flowering to within a couple of buds of the main framework, but this means that the decorative seed heads will not develop.

3. The most complicated group of large-flowered hybrids: those that produce large (or double), flowers in early summer on wood produced the previous year as well as smaller (single), flowers in late summer on new growth. Examples include 'Duchess of Edinburgh', 'Joan Picton', 'Wada's Primrose' and 'The President'. A simple way to treat them is to leave them unpruned (after the initial prune at planting), but to cut them right back every few years when they become straggly. With a good feed, they soon shoot up again and the only loss is one season's display of the early flowers.

   Alternatively, a renewal system can be followed, but only where the plant grows directly against a wall or fence (it would be very tricky to disentangle the pruned shoots from a shrub or other climber). Prune hard at planting and cut back the first season's growth by one half the following winter. In summer, after flowering, cut back about one-quarter of the mature (flowered) shoots to within 30cm (1ft) of the base of the plant.

4. Some large-flowered clematis, including 'Marie Boisselot', 'Henryi' and 'Hagley Hybrid', flower equally well on both old and young wood. Pruning of these is entirely optional. An unpruned specimen will come into flower earlier in the year, but if you want a later display (of

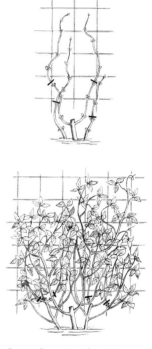

Spring-flowering clematis

Top: Initial hard pruning encourages the formation of several shoots. Each of these should be cut back by one half during the winter to ensure a strong framework.

Bottom: Further pruning is usually unnecessary, but if you need to keep the plant under tighter control, remove some of the flowered shoots immediately after flowering.

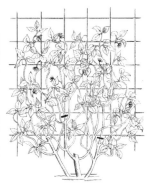

Large-flowered clematis
It is possible to prevent a
mature clematis becoming too
leggy by judicious pruning:
immediately after the last
flowering cut back roughly a
quarter of the flowered shoots
to a point where there are new
shoots. In this way the plant
can be controlled without the
loss of next season's flowers.

slightly smaller flowers), prune hard in
spring.

Lonicera

These can be grown perfectly well with no
pruning at all, but if you want or need to contain them, this is how to do it:

The vigorous *L. japonica* flowers on current growth. The hard edges left by a clip
over (severe, if necessary), in late spring
will quickly be softened by the emergence
of new growth which will bear flowers
later in the year.

Other honeysuckles, including *L. ×
americana, periclymenum, sempervirens* and *tragophylla*, flower on laterals produced from the
previous season's growth. If they become
too tangled, cut back some of the old,
weaker stems as well as a proportion of the
flowered shoots, to points where vigorous
new growth is appearing.

Climbing roses

The species and their close relatives are
mainly large, vigorous plants which need
space and require minimal pruning except
the removal of dead, damaged and diseased wood. At planting, remove weak
shoots and any which have been damaged.
These roses flower on wood produced the
previous summer: if the plant becomes
overcrowded, remove shoots which have
borne flowers as soon as the blooms have
faded. This will, unfortunately, spoil the
display of rosehips that is part of the charm
of the species roses, so keep pruning to a
minimum. *R. banksiae* reacts badly to any
pruning at all, tending to die back where it
has been cut.

The once-flowering ramblers flower
on laterals arising from the long shoots

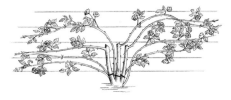

produced the previous year, so should be
pruned in summer, after flowering. Hard
pruning when they are planted will
encourage vigorous growth, so cut back
all the stems to about 30cm (1ft) from
the ground, making the cuts just above a
good sideways-pointing bud. In subsequent years, you should aim to leave a
well-balanced framework of long new
shoots (which will bear flowers the following year), by removing shoots which have
flowered. For some roses, such as 'Dorothy
Perkins', which produce plenty of new

Rambler roses
Top: At planting cut back all
the stems to about 30cm (1ft)
from the ground, making each
cut just above a good
sideways-pointing bud.

Centre: During the first summer
tie in the long shoots
horizontally as they grow;
they will bear flowers the
following year.

Bottom: In the late summer of
subsequent years the flowered
stems should be removed as
low down as possible.
Throughout the summer new
shoots will spring from the
base (to bear next year's
flowers): these also should be
trained horizontally.

shoots right from the base, this means cutting old wood back almost to the ground; with others, such as 'Albertine', which are less inclined to throw up new shoots from the base, cut back to where a good new shoot is growing.

The true, mainly repeat-flowering climbers must not be pruned hard at planting, because many are simply climbing sports of bush varieties and it is possible to make them revert to bushes if they are cut right back. Instead, remove only weak and damaged shoots. Train branches towards the horizontal while they are young and pliable. Winter pruning consists of cutting back flowered laterals to 15 cm (6 in) or so, and removing weak shoots. In summer, dead-heading back to promising buds or shoots, together with ample feeding, will encourage repeat flowering.

Repeat-flowering roses

Top: It is important to spread the branches towards the horizontal (although they will be less pliable than a rambler's whippy shoots) to encourage flowering along the length of each stem.

Bottom: Flowered laterals have been cut back during winter; during the summer the shoots are trained horizontally. Remove dead flowers or clusters of bloom by cutting back to strong buds or shoots, to encourage repeat flowering.

Wisteria

This is such a vigorous plant that it needs twice-yearly pruning to keep it in shape and bring it into flower.

The establishment of the main frame-

work is illustrated. Thereafter, cut back new side shoots to 15cm (6in) – four to six buds – in late summer, and shorten these further in winter to two to three buds per shoot to encourage the formation of flowering spurs.

Shrubs

Many shrubs, including *Abelia, Abutilon, Camellia, Carpenteria, Ceratostigma, Chaenomeles, Chimonanthus, Choisya, Convolvulus, Coronilla, Cotoneaster, Fremontodendron, Garrya, Hydrangea, Lagerstroemia, Lavatera, Lippia, Magnolia, Mahonia, Myrtus,*

Wisteria

Top: This good framework has resulted from the main stem being pruned at planting back to roughly 1m (3ft) from the ground. The new leader is tied vertically and the laterals trained towards the horizontal. During the following winter these three main shoots should be reduced by about one-third.

Centre: Next summer the new laterals are tied horizontally. Late in the growing season sub-laterals and surplus laterals are shortened to 15–23cm (6–9in).

Bottom: In subsequent summers cut back new side shoots (which may be long and tangled) to 15–23cm (6–9in). Over winter shorten each of these further to two–three buds.

Buddleia
Pruning is simple: cut back
flowered shoots in spring to a
pair of strong buds (*top*). If the
plant becomes congested in
later years, cut out some of the
inward-pointing stems to let in
light and air (*bottom*).

Pittosporum, *Teucrium* and *Viburnum* need
hardly any pruning because they rarely
produce replacement shoots from the base
of lower branches. It is, however, important
to create a good framework after planting. To this end, remove weak or crossing shoots during the first couple of
winters. Thereafter, the only pruning
should be the removal of dead, damaged
or diseased wood.

Shrubs which flower on shoots produced the previous season should be
pruned after flowering to give space to the
shoots which will bear flowers the following year. These include *Buddleia alternifolia*,
Cytisus, *Forsythia*, *Jasminum nudiflorum* and
Kerria. Simply cut back flowered stems to
vigorous young shoots further down. At
the same time, take out any weak shoots.
In later years, the plant may become overcrowded, so cut out about one-quarter of
the oldest stems right at the base.

Shrubs which flower late in summer on
growth produced during the current season are easy to deal with. Cut them back in
spring. The degree to which an individual
plant should be cut back depends on both
the plant and what you want it to do. Some
such as *Fuchsia*, *Perovskia* and *Phygelius*, are
often killed to the ground by frost over
winter, so the dead stems should be cut off
in spring. Others are hardy enough to
make a woody framework, the size of
which you can determine: *Buddleia* (except
B. alternifolia) falls into this category.

Shrubs which can be trained more
closely to a wall include the following
special examples:

Ceanothus grow fast and it is vital to
spread the lateral shoots regularly to
encourage them to cover the wall evenly.

These plants, like many others, produce a
proportion of shoots which grow directly
away from the wall (breastwood), and
these must be cut back. If pruning is
neglected, *Ceanothus* will quickly bulge
away from a wall and become vulnerable to
damage by wind and snow. In any case,
they resent being cut back to older, hard
wood, so an old misshapen specimen
should be removed; it cannot properly be
renovated. Clip over the whole plant after
flowering, to keep it neat.

Pyracantha is often grown close to a wall,
so should be trained like a *Ceanothus*, by
tying in new shoots while still young and
pliable, and removing breastwood. Do not
cut back after flowering, though, or there
will be no berries.

Chaenomeles give a satisfactory display
with no pruning at all, because they produce side shoots freely, but to maximize
flowering you should prune in both summer and autumn. In summer, new shoots
should be shortened to four to six leaves: in
autumn, the secondary shoots arising from
the summer-pruned shoots can be reduced
to two to three leaves so that flowering
spurs are encouraged. This also reveals the
decorative fruit. The spurs will eventually
become congested and need thinning in
winter.

Fruit

The three main shapes for wall-trained
fruit are the cordon, the espalier and the
fan. A beginner might like to buy ready-
trained specimens in the first instance and
then, having gained confidence pruning
these, to progress to the more satisfying
task of training a tree from a one-year-old
maiden plant or whip. All wall-trained

fruit will need a firm system of horizontal wires attached to the wall at intervals of 30cm (1ft) or so.

CORDON

This is a single- or multiple-stemmed plant often trained at an oblique angle. Training the plant at an angle restricts its vigour and keeps it within bounds to facilitate pruning and harvesting. Plant a maiden tree and secure it to wires at an angle of 45°. Do not cut the leader, but prune any side shoots to four buds. The following winter, cut the laterals to four buds and sub-laterals to two buds. It is best not to allow the plant to fruit at an early age, so remove any flower buds the following spring,

making sure you leave the basal rosette of leaves. In summer, prune laterals to three leaves from the base and sub-laterals to 2.5cm (1in). If, for any reason you do not do this, find time to do it the following winter. Thereafter, continue this spur pruning in summer and winter, and thin out congested spur systems every few years. Stop the leader only when the plant reaches the height you want.

ESPALIER

An espaliered plant has a central stem which gives rise to horizontal fruiting branches at regular intervals. Beginning with a maiden tree, cut off the stem just above the lowest training wire, making sure that there are three promising buds below. The following summer, tie the top shoot vertically and the other two at angles of about 45°, fixing them to canes attached to the wires. In winter, carefully lower the side branches to the horizontal and cut them back by one-third, to a down-pointing bud. The vertical shoot should be cut above the next wire, leaving three more good buds to make the next year's leader and two new arms. This process is repeated until the espalier reaches the required height, when only two stems are allowed to make the final horizontal arms. Side shoots on the vertical and horizontal stems should be summer pruned to five leaves and shortened again in winter in the same manner as for cordons. Rub or cut off any shoots which try to grow towards the wall.

FAN

This is a simple pattern to create, although it is important to make sure that the stems are evenly spread so that they are properly exposed to sunlight. A maiden tree should

Cordon

Top: Secure the maiden tree to a cane attached to wires at 45°. The side shoots are pruned to four buds. The following winter prune laterals to four buds and sub-laterals to two buds.

Bottom: A sad, but necessary, task the second spring is to remove the flower buds to prevent the tree diverting energy into fruit production. In summer prune the sub-laterals to 2.5cm (1in); the laterals also are pruned – to three leaves from the base.

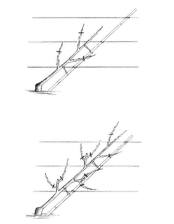

Espalier

Top: Cut the maiden tree to just above the lowest wire.

Centre: The framework at the end of the first summer: shoots tied to canes on horizontal wires.

Bottom: During the winter gently pull the shoots to lie horizontally and shorten them by one-third. Cut the leader just above the second wire. This process is repeated in subsequent years until there are as many tiers of branches as wires.

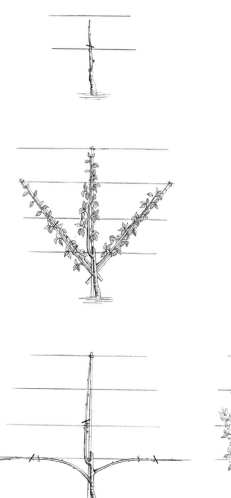

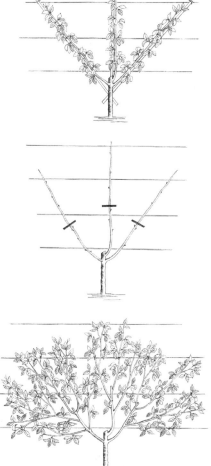

Fan

Top: Strong shoots resulting from the initial pruning are tied to canes.

Centre: The following winter cut the stems back to about 30cm (1ft) to encourage the growth of more laterals.

Bottom: A well-trained fan which fills its allotted space. Plums, damsons and cherries must have their older and crossing branches removed to leave space for new growth. Peaches must have their fruit-bearing branches renewed every year: to do this, remove all side shoots except two (one at the base and one at the tip) during the summer; in the autumn cut out the fruited branch and tie in the basal shoot which will fruit the following year.

be shortened to 30cm (1ft) or so and the resulting strong shoots tied to canes fixed to the wires. The following winter, these strong shoots can be shortened to about 30cm (1ft) to encourage the formation of

more branches. Tie these in symmetrically to fill the available space. Plums, damsons and, to a lesser extent, cherries, are all susceptible to a fungal disease called Silver Leaf. This enters the tree through wounds, but the risk of infection is much less in the summer months when the tree is in active growth. To reduce the chances of losing a tree, prune only during the summer and avoid making large wounds.

GRAPEVINES

Grapevines need a lot of attention during the growing season to reduce the prolific growth and encourage yields of good quality fruit. A grapevine may be grown as a cordon, an espalier or in a less formal arrangement, but whatever the shape of the plant, the grapes are borne on current growth. For grapes of the best quality, allow only one bunch to develop on each shoot. In early winter, after the leaves have fallen, cut back the side shoots that carried fruit, leaving two buds at the base. It is important to do this before the sap starts to rise in very early spring, to avoid excessive bleeding of the cuts. In spring, keep the stronger of the two shoots and stop it just beyond the two leaves above the first bunch of flowers. Some of the young grapes must also be removed to allow the others to reach a good size.

Plants on retaining walls

The alpine, spreading types, such as *Aubrieta* and *Iberis*, should be clipped back after flowering to keep them neat. Lavender needs similar treatment. Using shears, cut off the faded flower heads and about 2.5cm (1 in) of the growth below to make a rounded cushion. Doing this every year ensures that the plant stays as compact as is reasonable: lavender does not respond well to being cut right back to old wood, so leggy specimens cannot usually be restored.

Grapevine

The Double Guyot system is a traditional method of training an outdoor grapevine.

Top: After initial hard pruning to 15cm (6in) a single stem is allowed to develop and any side shoots removed. In early winter the leader is cut back to about 60cm (2ft) from the ground above three good buds. The following summer three shoots are trained vertically.

Centre top: In winter the two side shoots are gently pulled down, tied in and cut back to 1m (3ft) or so. The leader is again cut to above three good buds.

Centre bottom: Fruiting laterals have grown from the horizontal rods and the three central shoots have been tied in vertically. The fruiting laterals should be thinned if they are closer than 15cm (6in) and must be stopped at the top wire.

Below: In early winter the rods which bore fruit are removed and the new shoots lowered as replacements. The main stem is shortened to above three good buds as before and the whole process is repeated.

· USEFUL BOOKS ·

Although I would not recommend that anyone build a wall solely from written instructions, *DIY Guide, Outdoors and Gardens* by Albert Jackson and David Day (Collins, 1986), covers basic techniques for walls and fences, as well as other outdoor structures. General inspiration can be gleaned from Diana Saville's *Walled Gardens, their planning and design* (Batsford, 1982) which is comprehensive and entertaining. There is also a selection of pieces on rock and wall gardening in Clare Best and Caroline Boisset's anthology, *Leaves from the Garden* (John Murray, 1987).

Useful reference books include: *The Gardeners' Illustrated Encyclopaedia of Climbers and Wall Shrubs* by Brian Davis (Viking, 1990) and the beautiful but expensive *Classic Roses* by Peter Beales (Collins Harvill, 1985). *Clematis* by Christopher Lloyd (Viking, revised 1989) makes good reading as well as being invaluable reference. A. M. Clevely's *Topiary* (Collins, 1988) is excellent on formal hedges. I have also enjoyed an older book *Hedges for Farm and Garden* by J. L. Beddall (Faber and Faber, 1950). *The Complete Guide to Fruit Growing* by Peter Blackburn-Maze (Crowood, 1988) is comprehensive; Christopher Brickell's *Pruning* (Mitchell

Beazley, 1979) is extremely clear and easy to follow; it covers hedges and many shrubs as well as climbers and fruit. *The Integrated Garden* by A. M. Clevely (Barrie and Jenkins, 1988) is good on fruit cultivation with specific suggestions on how fruit (and other edibles) can be combined with 'ornamental' subjects.

Less specialized gardening books which I would not be without include the newly revised *Perennial Garden Plants* by Graham Stuart Thomas (Dent, 1990). *Hilliers' Manual of Trees and Shrubs* (Hillier Nurseries (Winchester) Ltd, 5th ed. 1981) is also vital – it includes a section on climbers. Also useful is Graham Stuart Thomas' *The Art of Planting* (Dent, 1984) which contains extensive lists of plants that should flower at the same time. *The Well-Tempered Garden* by Christopher Lloyd (Viking, revised 1985) is a classic. I also recommend Robin Lane Fox's *Better Gardening* (R & L, 1982); it teaches selectivity when choosing any type of plant. Finally, Penelope Hobhouse's *Colour in Your Garden* (Collins, 1985) is a beautifully organized reference book which arranges plants by colour and season and is invaluable when composing planting schemes.

·PLANT SUPPLIERS·

UK PLANT SUPPLIERS

It is not possible in a limited space to give an exhaustive list of plant suppliers so the following is a selection of useful nurseries. In case of difficulty in tracking down a particular plant, the book to consult is *The Plant Finder* (Headmain Ltd for the Hardy Plant Society, published annually), which lists 45,000 plants.

General Nurseries

Blooms of Bressingham, Diss Norfolk IP22 2AB
Hillier Nurseries (Winchester) Ltd, Ampfield House, Ampfield, Romsey, Hants SO51 9PA
Scotts Nurseries, Merriott, Somerset TA16 5PL

Specialist Nurseries

CLIMBERS

J. Bradshaw and Son, Busheyfield Nursery, Herne Bay, Kent CT6 7LJ – holds national collection of climbing Lonicera
Fisks Clematis, Westleton, Saxmundham, Suffolk IP17 3AJ
Great Dixter Nurseries, Northiam, Rye, E. Sussex TN31 6PH
Pennells Nurseries, Newark Road, South Hykeham, Lincoln LN6 9NT
Stone House Cottage Nurseries, Stone, Kidderminster, Worcs DY10 4BG
Treasures of Tenbury Ltd, Burford House Gardens, Tenbury Wells, Worcs WR15 8HQ
Whitehouse Ivies, Hylands Farm, Rectory Road, Tolleshunt Knights, Maldon, Essex CM9 8EZ

ROSES

David Austin, Bowling Green Lane, Albrighton Lane, Albrighton, Wolverhampton WV7 3HB
Peter Beales Roses, London Road, Attleborough, Norfolk NR17 1AY

FRUIT AND VINE

Cranmore Vine Nursery, Yarmouth, Isle of Wight PO41 0XS
Deacons Nursery, Godshill, Isle of Wight PO38 3HW
Eden Nurseries, Rectory Lane, Old Bolingbroke, Spilsby, Lincs PE23 4EY – English apples
Yearlstone Vineyard, Chilverton, Coldridge, Crediton, Devon EX17 6BH

PLANTS FOR RETAINING WALLS

R. G. M. Cawthorne, Lower Dalton's Nursery, Swanley Village, Swanley, Kent BR8 7AU – 450 violas and violettas, national collection of violas
Unusual Plants, Beth Chatto Gardens, Elmstead Market, Colchester, Essex CO7 7DB
J. & E. Parker-Jervis, Marten's Hall Farm, Longworth, Abingdon OX13 5EP – cottage plants

HEDGING

Buckingham Nurseries, 14 Tingewick Road, Buckingham MK18 4AE – bare-rooted and container-grown hedge plants
Langley Boxwood Nursery, Langley Court, Rake, Liss, Hants GU33 7JL – *Buxus* spp. and cultivars, topiary and hedging
R. V. Roger Ltd, The Nurseries, Pickering, N. Yorks YO18 7HG

US PLANT SUPPLIERS

General (climbers, shrubs & rock plants)

Garden Place, 6780 Heisley Rd., P.O. Box 388, Mentor OH 44061-0388
Holbrook Farm & Nursery, Rt. 2, Box 223B, Fletcher, NC 28732
Lamb Nurseries, E. 101 Sharp Ave., Spokane, WA 99202
Nature's Garden, Rt. 1, Box 488, Beaverton, OR 97007
Park Seed Co., Cokesbury Rd., Greenwood, SC 29647-0001
Siskiyou Rare Plant Nursery, 2825 Cummings Rd., Medford, OR 97501
Wayside Gardens, Garden Lane, Hodges, SC 29692-0001
White Flower Farm, Rt. 63, Litchfield, CT 06759-0050

Specialist Nurseries

ROSES

Antique Rose Emporium, Rt. 5, Box 143, Brenham, TX 77833
Pickering Nurseries Inc., 670 Kingston Rd., Pickering, Ontario L1V 1A6
Roses of Yesterday and Today, 802 Brown's Valley Rd., Watsonville, CA 95076

FRUIT

Kelly Brother Nurseries Inc, 100 Maple St., Dansville, NY 14437
Southmeadow Fruit Gardens, Lakeside, MI 49116
Stark Brothers Nurseries and Orchards, Box 2281F, Louisiana, MO 63353

• ACKNOWLEDGEMENTS •

PHOTOGRAPHS

Neil Campbell-Sharp: p. 89
Charles O. Cresson: pp. 44 (top left), 45,
55 (top left & right), 62 (left)
Eric Crichton: pp. 52 (below), 69
Jerry Harpur: pp. i, 9
(top/designer/Anne Griot, Los Angeles;
below/designer/Robin Williams), 11
(below/designer/Kevin Newman), 13
(Beth Chatto), 21 (right), 24 (top
left/designer/Ragna Goddard; top
right/designer/Edwina von Gal, NYC;
below/designer/Gus Lieber, Long Island),
28 (Hazlebury Manor, Wilts), 31
(left/designer/Bruce Kelly, New York), 35
(top), 41 (designer/John Patrick,
Melbourne), 46 (below), 47
(designer/Lanning Roper), 49, 60 (below
left/Hazleby House, Berks);

(below right/designer/Michael Balston),
62 (right), 98 (left),
101 (left/designer/Penny Crawshaw)
Lorraine Johnson: pp. 50 (right), 54
(below), 57, 82 (left)
Andrew Lawson: p. 46 (top)
Marianne Majerus: pp. ii, 6, 11 (top), 15
(all), 17 (all), 25, 27 (below), 29, 31
(right), 32 (top left & right), 34, 35
(below), 38, 39, 42, 43, 44 (right above &
below), 50 (left), 51, 52 (top), 53, 54
(top), 55 (below), 56, 59, 60 (top left &
right), 65, 66, 68, 71, 72, 75, 76, 78, 79,
81, 82 (right), 85, 86 (all), 90, 93, 94, 95,
97, 98 (right), 101 (top), 103, 104
(below), 107, 110, 111, 112
Jerry Pavia pp. 21 (left top & below), 23,
27 (top), 32 (below left & right), 64
Joanne Pavia pp. 48, 104 (top)

INDEX

·INDEX·